一套推动和普及中国动漫游戏
教育及产业发展的优秀教材

教育部全国职业教育与成人教育教学用书行业规划教材

“十二五”全国高校动漫游戏专业骨干课程权威教材

专家委员会

指导单位
中国动画学会
中国图形图像学会
中国视协卡通艺委会
连环漫画研究会

总策划
北京电影学院动画学院

总主编
孙立军

出版策划
孙立军
杨绥华
钱晓彬
邹华跃
黄梅琪
蒋湘群
申　彪
吴清平
赵　武

整体企划
赵　武

张会军　（全国政协委员、北京电影学院院长）
孙立军　（北京电影学院动画学院院长）
高福安　（中国传媒大学副校长）
廖祥忠　（中国传媒大学动画学院副院长）
肖永亮　（北京师范大学艺术与传媒学院副院长）
王　钢　（同济大学传播与艺术学院动画系主任）
林　超　（中国美术学院传媒动画学院副院长）
于少非　（中央戏曲学院新媒体艺术系主任）
晓　欧　（中央美术学院城市设计学院动画系主任）
吴冠英　（清华大学美术学院动画实验室主任）
戴铁郎　（著名动画导演）
余为政　（台南艺术学院动画研究所所长）
朱德庸　（著名漫画家）
黄玉郎　（著名漫画家）
严定宪　（著名动画导演）
王庸声　（连环漫画研究会会长）
余培侠　（中央电视台青少中心主任）
沈向洋　（微软亚洲研究院院长）
凯西·史密斯（美国南加州大学动画系主任）
凯文·盖格（美国迪斯尼公司著名动画导演）
谢福顺　（新加坡南洋大学计算机工程学院院长副教授）
田　丰　（新加坡南洋理工大学电脑工程学院助理教授）
马志辉　（香港理工大学设计学院副院长）
赖淑玲　（台湾岭东科技大学设计学院院长）
韩永燮　（韩国祥明大学艺术大学教授/画家）

（以上排名不分先后）

21 Century High Education Textbooks for Animation, Comics and Game

“十二五”全国高校动漫游戏专业骨干课程权威教材

动漫游戏专业高等教育教材专家组/审定

Animation English Course

影视动画英语教程

编著/阳泽宇　于志恒等

审校/王诗戈

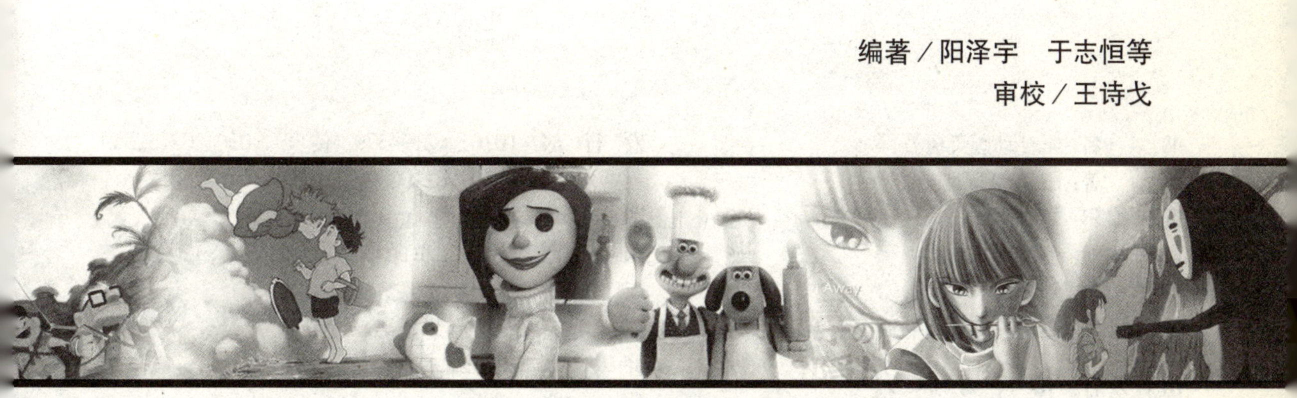

海洋出版社

2011年·北京

内容简介

动画专业英语是各级动画专业学生的必修课，本书根据动画专业英语教学大纲编写，适应当前动漫教学特点，符合动漫教育发展趋势。

全书分为三大部分：基础篇、人物篇、拓展篇，每篇分设六章，内容涵盖了动画专业的各个方面，包括动画历史、动画制作基础、著名动画公司、知名动画人、经典作品、最新动画技术、动画产业等。课文部分（Text）选取了长短适度，难易适中的文章，既能提高学生在动画专业英语方面的读写能力，也不会因为文章过难而影响学生的学习兴趣。每篇课文后还精心设置了单词与短语（Words and Phrases）、注释（Notes）、练习（Comprehensive Questions）、扩展阅读（Further Reading）、学习网址（Web Links）等项目，帮助学生扎实掌握关键知识点，快速提高专业英语能力。

本书是动画专业教材，适用于动画相关专业各个层次的教育教学，同时也可作为动画专业工作者和爱好者的自学用书。

图书在版编目(CIP)数据

影视动画英语教程/阳泽宇，于志恒编著．—北京：海洋出版社，2011.4

ISBN 978-7-5027-7973-3

Ⅰ.①影…　Ⅱ.①阳…②于…　Ⅲ.①动画片—英语—高等学校—教材　Ⅳ.①H31

中国版本图书馆 CIP 数据核字（2011）第 040354 号

书　　名：影视动画英语教程
编　　著：阳泽宇　于志恒等
责任编辑：赵　武
责任校对：肖新民
责任印制：刘志恒
排　　版：海洋计算机图书输出中心　晓阳
出版发行：海洋出版社
地　　址：北京市海淀区大慧寺路 8 号（705 室）
100081
技术支持：（010）62100052

发 行 部：（010）62174379（传真）（010）62132549
（010）62100075（邮购）（010）62173651
网　　址：www.oceanpress.com.cn
承　　印：北京海洋印刷厂印刷
版　　次：2011 年 4 月第 1 版
2011 年 4 月第 1 次印刷
开　　本：787mm×1092mm　1/16
印　　张：11.5
字　　数：260 千字
印　　数：1～3000 册
定　　价：38.00 元

出版者的话

伴随着互联网技术和CG技术日新月异的发展，动漫游戏产业的前景给每个置身其中的人带来了无限的遐想，全世界影视动画、动漫、游戏行业不断制造的财富故事，特别是欧美发达国家、邻国韩日动漫已经成为其国民经济支柱的现实，为中国动漫游戏产业展示着绚丽的色彩。巨大的市场空间及需求，新媒体动画技术的发展，给中国动漫游戏产业再创昔日“中国学派”的辉煌带来了一次难得的历史性机遇，中国动漫游戏产业为“赶上了好时候”而兴奋不已，整个产业正在涌动着激情的创业热潮。

人才是企业及产业发展的“源动力”，已经成为共识。但是目前动漫游戏人才的数量和质量，离产业的需求有相当差距，这无疑使我国快速发展的动漫游戏产业遭遇瓶颈。人才现实的需求，直接催生了近些年来中国动画教育的蓬勃发展，无论是本科、高职还是各类培训班新生人数及在校人数每年都在快速增长。但是动漫游戏毕竟是新生事物，面对这样的新行业、新技术，如何快速提高“教学水平”，为产业培养及输送既有创意又有实操执行能力的“真人才”，是我们教育工作者面临的一个全新挑战。教学的核心是“课程的设置和教材的编写”，一套高标准的“动漫游戏专业高等教育教材”的推出已经成为各类专业院校的普遍需求。

由北京电影学院动画学院、中国动画学会及海洋出版社等知名机构共同发起和组建的“动漫游戏专业高等教育教材编委会”，组织国内优秀的一线老师历时三年，搜集并整理了大量欧美、韩国、日本等优秀的动画游戏学院的课程设置、教材等教学资料，广泛征求了海内外教育专家、技术专家的各类意见，结合国内的实际情况，编写了这套《“十二五”全国高校动漫游戏专业骨干课程权威教材》，力图全面展示“最核心的动漫游戏理论”、“最新的技术”、“最典型的项目应用“，为国内动漫游戏专业提供一套标准的通用教材。只有建立了这样一种规范和标准，才能使来自各个不同的院校毕业生、在日常的工作中有一种共同的知识底蕴，才会有共同的语言去“对话、沟通”，这样的合作正是中国动漫游戏产业迅速做强做大的根本，否则，我们的动漫游戏可能没有产业，只有作坊。

中国的动漫游戏教育刚刚开始，动漫游戏教材又是一个日常日新的巨大工程，“动漫游戏专业高等教育教材编委会”则是一个开放的平台，因此，衷心希望国内外专家，特别是身在教育最前线的老师加入到我们的策划与编写队伍中来，“众人拾柴火焰高”，让我们共同为推动中国的动漫游戏教育及产业的发展贡献自己的心力和才智。时值本套教材出版不久前，国家有关部门连续出台《关于发展我国影视动画产业的若干意见》、《关于实施“中国民族网络游戏出版工程”的通知》及在北京电影学院等著名高校建立“影视动画原创基地”等重大决策，全力规划并支持动漫游戏产业的发展，甚是欣慰，机会真的来了。

动漫游戏专业高等教育教材编委会

教育部全国职业教育与成人教育教学用书行业规划教材

“十二五”全国高校动漫游戏专业骨干课程权威教材

编写委员会

从书总序

进入崭新的21世纪，中国的动画事业将如何发展?

尤其在美国、日本的电影动画得到普遍认同和接受，成为举足轻重的类型片以及其动漫画产业蒸蒸日上成为重要的支柱产业的今天，中国动画产业在各方面都存在着有目共睹的差距，甚至在很多领域存在着诸多的空白!

中国动画如何在严峻的形势下找到属于自己的出路，再现“中国学派”的辉煌，这些挑战无疑都已经现实地摆在我们的面前。而对于每一个动画从业者，或者是正准备投身于动画事业的人来说，更是责无旁贷!

说到我们的动画创作，虽在改革开放后取得了长足的进步和发展，但是与先进国家的差距却已经日益明显地加大。这当中存在着多方面的因素，最为突出的是我国缺乏大批优秀的动画创作性人才，而发展动画教育则又是人才形成的根本保证。

要真正发展我国的动画事业，毋庸置疑首先要关注我们动画教育如何真正地完善。虽然我国的动画教育早从20世纪的50年代就已经在北京电影学院等院校中开始，也培养了一批优秀的动画人才，但是随着整个动画的发展，动画教育也显然面临着新的挑战。随着社会各界对于动画事业发展的日益关注，全国各地院校纷纷建立了动画专业，出现了除研究生、本科、大专院校以外，还包括中专、短期培训等等各种层次的教育形式，为更多有志于在动画领域发展的青年提供了大量的学习机会。中国动画教育正表现出极好的发展态势。但是，出于历史、经济等各方面原因，我们的动画教育一直以来都存在着缺乏系统、科学和连续性的弊病；而在课程设置、教学安排等方面也都未能真正实现一个完整的教育体系。不仅如此，我们的动画教育还没有一套完备的、科学的、体系化的专业教材，显然在很大程度上制约着我国动画教育的发展。一套高水准的专业动画教材已经成为我国动画高等教育的普遍需求，但是我们也要看到，要编写这样的一套教材，难度之大可想而知。不仅要将授课内容和动画创作的精华浓缩在有限的文字和图片中，还要用我们比较熟悉的学习方式去布置各种重要的知识点，而且还要将各国动画大师的创作经验以及优秀作品的成功所在进行理论化、科学化的归纳，并结合到行之有效的教学中……这显然更是难上加难。

北京电影学院动画专业教育经过多年的教学积累和实践总结，逐步形成了一套行之有效、具备突出特点的课程安排和教学体系。为了让我们积累的一些教学经验与更多的兄弟院校分享，为了动画人才能够在更为系统和科学的教育中茁壮成长，从而培养更多更好的优秀动画工作者，我们开始筹备这套国内最为全面的《“十二五”全国高校动漫游戏专业骨干课程权威教材》。

为了保证本系列教材的科学性和严肃性，我们组织了上百名以北京电影学院动画学院为主体的优秀教师和国内外专家、教授（其中大多都经历过大量的动画创作实践并且参与了动画教学，具备着丰富的教学经验和个人积累），编写历时多年。因此，从组织的人力、物力、数量以及时间的投入等角度来说，本套动画教材可以说是中国有史以来最大型、最权威的动画教材。

在整套教材的安排上，我们的主导思路是将理论建设和实践操作相结合，强调优秀动画作品的理论总结和动画创作的可操作性两个方面。教材关注当前各国动画的最新发展，将动画的创作理念、艺术创作方式和科技手段等方面有机结合，内容包含了动画创作和各种基础训练、专业训练、各类技法以及动画的影片分析、动画剧作训练、动画大师研究……所以在规模上、系统性上都是我国动画教材的首创，我们本着“依靠理论来指导实践，依靠实践来丰富理论”的整体设想在如何突出整个教学体系、课程安排等角度上编写了本系列教材。

本系列教材的编写过程中，在突出教材实用性的同时，我们坚持“观念新、写作手法新、实例新”的理念，一方面在写作上突破死板和教条的语言，将各个学习点从基础到不断深化的过程体现得活泼而生动；另一方面，突出最新的实例来指导教学，拉近知识与生活的距离，让学生在最新的资讯中以最简单的方式获得知识。

整套系列教材从整体策划、收集整理资料，到作者撰写、编辑出版，历时多年，工程浩大，凝聚了许多人的心血，处处体现了工作者脚踏实地的严谨作风，表现出对中国动画教育事业的执着热情。在此，我再次感谢为本套教材付出劳动和努力的每一个人！真诚感谢他们为中国动画教育所作的卓越贡献。

衷心希望此套系列丛书能够在一定程度上“推动我国动画教育的纵深发展，促进我国动画人才的成熟壮大，开创我国的动画创作更为辉煌的局面”的目标，作出我们力所能及的贡献。

当然，由于时间的紧迫以及动画本身创作的复杂性，在编写过程中肯定存在着诸多的不足和纰漏，恳请广大专家、同行批评指正。

本系列丛书不仅可以作为高等院校动画专业的专业教材，同时也适合动画公司的创作人员以及动画爱好者自学使用。

丛书主编

北京电影学院动画学院院长

本书序

应泽宇君之邀为本书作序，我欣然领命。

谈起中国动画，国人每每气短，历数动画“中国学派”曾经的辉煌岁月，以及在世界动画界缔造获奖神话而生豪迈之情的同时，又感慨中国当下动画在日美动画强势逼迫之下的困窘和令人沮丧，一副恨铁不成钢的模样。而有雄心的动画人，面对种种苛责，则常感到好像以贻误中国动画的带罪之身忝列这个行业，每每惴惴然愧疚不已。

其实，就业界而言，我们中国当下的动画人是有骨气的人，是有爱国心的人。从“视金石”到“水晶石”，从北京到西安、长沙、上海、苏州、杭州、常州，从长三角到珠三角，我们已有一大群动画人，他们大多三四十岁，在好莱坞、在香港、在国内做加工片，经过一二十年的摸爬滚打，已经积累了丰富的管理、制作经验、也深谙市场规律，最为重要的是，这些中坚和砥柱是有理想的人，是敢于为梦想而搏命的人，他们以一种悲壮的姿态搴旗前行，每人都率领着一个几十到几百人的团队，在埋头做事，在披坚执锐地冲锋，在向好莱坞叫阵，用自己的作品来回答评论界、动漫迷和整个社会的诘问。

所以我认为中国动画所受的指责和动画人的愧疚在21世纪第二个十年必将为扬眉吐气所代替。在我撰写和发表的各类文章中，我始终如一的观点是：随着中国影视在21世纪第一个十年的全面中兴，中国动画在21世纪第二个十年一定中兴！一定会刷新享有世界声誉的动画“中国学派”曾经写就的辉煌！

动画产业被誉为21世纪最具发展潜力的朝阳产业，我国将力争在未来5至10年内，跻身世界动漫大国和强国行列。中国动画产业近年发展迅猛，有赖于国家政策的扶持和各级部门的重视，北京、上海、杭州、大连、深圳、广州、青岛等各地纷纷建立动漫产业基地，民营动漫企业发展很快，游戏动漫人才成为市场上最紧俏的人才之一。

鉴于此，各个高校纷纷设立了动画专业，许多相关专业学生和从业者也转战游戏动漫业。现有的3D软件不断更新换代，具备了更多先进的功能，不少喜好动漫的业余级“粉丝”也加入到了动漫制作的大军中来，这是一个可喜的现象。技术的发展降低了动漫行业的准入门槛，但是将来要在这个行业取得成功，仍然必须具备造型绘画的能力和讲故事的能力。其实，动漫除在制作工艺和流程上与过去有不同之外，对动画人才的素质要求和过去本质上是一样的。需要对这个行业的历史和成功的经验进行学习与总结，需要理论与实践并重，高校管理者和一线从教人员也已清醒地认识到了这个问题。

进入新世纪以来，中国各个高校纷纷开设动画专业，每年有几十万学生就读，但动画教学的模式和课程设置却还在摸着石头过河。甫一开始，过多的强调技能技巧的训练而忽视理论学习，结果导致毕业的学生动手制作能力强而创意编导能力弱，这也是我国近年动画在编创方面颇受批评的原因之一。现在这一情况有所改观，随着大量的影视、美术、文学、历史、文化研究类的学者介入这一领域，动画理论课的教学也起了可喜的变化，动画概论、动画视听语言、动画作品分析、动画编剧、世界动画史、动画大师研究、动画美学这些课程的教材也由原先比较简陋的状态变得更有深度了。此外一些新的课程也陆续开设，如动画制作管理、动画专业英语等。此类课程的设立，标志着动画教学的日趋成熟和完善。

我们既需要在业界披坚执锐，搴纛前行的行业先锋，也需要在教育行业兢兢业业，扎实做事的教师精英，为这个行业培养后备力量，不断补充新鲜血液。而在教育界，也涌现了一大批热爱动画，视动画教育为安身立命之所在的青年人，他们是动画教育界的新锐力量，他们或一边教学一边参与动画创作，或博览群书，撷英择珠，一边教学一边著书立说，总结国内外成功经验，将这些前辈们的成果介绍给如饥似渴的80后、90后学子，为中国动画培养更为年轻的后备力量。

阳泽宇君就是这类在为中国动画教育踏踏实实做事的青年人之一，他学美术出身，由于英语功底好，又长于思辨，对动画史论研究方面颇有造诣，长期以来一直担当世界动画史、动画大师研究、动画专业英语课程的教学。他把多年来在一线教学中遇到的问题进行了梳理，将收集积攒的大量的教学资料进行了归纳总结，组织了几位在动画理论研究和创作方面既有建树，英语功底又比较好的同仁编撰了这本教材。

这本教材精心选取了英文资料组成三个篇章：基础篇、人物篇和拓展篇。基础篇主要介绍动画的制作原理、写作原则等内容；人物篇主要选取了一些有代表性的动画大师的访谈录；拓展篇主要介绍了世界著名的动画电影奖项、动画教育和动画工业等相关内容。各个板块之间具有极强的逻辑层次关系，成为一个有关动画专业基础知识及史论知识的集成。这样编排，不但使学生掌握了动画专业英语专门术语，同时又能对动画概论、中外动画史、动画视听语言、动画大师研究等理论课程知识的学习形成了一个有益的补充，可为学生将来阅读动画外文通俗读物和专业刊物，了解最新动画资讯，学习国外先进的理念和制作技术打下坚实的语言基础。

本书另外一个特点就是所选英文资料难度适中，从易到难逐渐展开，既不是很浅显，也不是晦涩难懂，适合动画专业学生特点。

海洋出版社对中国动画教育是有贡献的，它当年出版的中国第一套高等院校动画专业系列，教材解决了前些年国内急需动画教材的燃眉之急，由北京电影学院动画学院编撰的教材供不应求，成为早期动画学子的入门“圣经”。海洋出版社至今在动画教材的出版方面一直向纵深方面发展，组织有志于斯的老中青学者和一线创作人员撰写了一部又一部高质量的教材，使莘莘学子受益。海洋出版社给国内诸多出版社树立了榜样，而榜样是有号召力的，随之而起的国内众多出版社也相继推出了成套的动画系列教材。

前辈潜心著述，培养和影响着年轻一代对动画的深厚感情，使他们甘愿把美好的青春祭献给动画，薪火相传，正是有了他们的青灯照壁、恒兀兀以穷年，才使中国动画学术著作和教材的出版呈现了百花齐放，百家争鸣的可喜局面。

本书作为百花之一束，相信各位读者都会喜欢它，祝大家开卷获益。

同济大学电影研究所执行所长　杨晓林

2011年元月于同济大学电影学院

体例说明

1. 每篇课文由课文（Text）、单词和短语（Words and Phrases）、注释（Notes）、练习（Comprehensive Questions）、扩展阅读（Further Reading）五部分组成。划线词汇为生词和短语，在“Words and Phrases”中解释；有数字标注的是动画专业名词，在“Notes”部分进行讲解。

Text

Beginners(2)

Background Design[1]

A **production designer**[2] or background designer is respon
designs. A background painter will paint a few key backgr
overseas to be matched by other painters painting additional ba
animation production is done in the United States <u>due to</u> the

Words and Phrases

due to
　　由于

refine　[ri'fain]
　　v. 精炼，提纯；改善

Notes

1. **background design 动画背景设计**：通常以叠层的形式置于动画
会置于之前。

Further Reading

◎ ***The Illusion of Life: Disney Animation***

Author: Ollie Johnston

Publisher: Disney Editions; Rev Sub edition (1995)

2. 斜体：所有电影电视片名用斜体字标出，以便于查找应用。

weren't like anyone we'd seen before. ***Finding Nemo***[4] was so moving and took the studio to new heights of popularity. ***The Incredibles***[5] was the most exciting thing they'd ever done. ***Cars***[6] made us feel both warm and nostalgic. ***Ratatouille***[7] was so classic. And *WALL-E* was so unique. If we're picking up our favorite Pixar film, that is easy for me: ***Monsters Inc***[8]. **Pete Docter's**[9] first

3. 生词的解释主要参考了中国人民大学出版社的《21世纪大英汉词典》(2003)，着重解释词语在课文语境中的意思。

general term　　通用术语，常用术语；总称

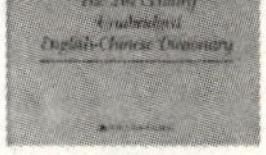

general supplies【军事】一般补给品
general support【军事】全般支援
general-support rocket system【军械】全般支援火箭系统
General System of Preference 普通优惠制
general system theory 一般系统论
general term【数学】通项，一般项
general theory of relativity【物理学】广义相对论〔1930~1935〕
general transduction 一般传导(作用)
general war【军事】全面战争
general will（体现或表达集体利益的）共同意志
gen·er·ant /ˈdʒenərənt/ *adj*. 1. 产生的；发生的 2.【数学】母点的，母线的，母面的 —*n*. 1. 发生器 2.【数学】

4. 专业术语注释当中如有比较重要的词汇在各篇文章中重复出现，用参见"chapter x-x"标明。

11. *Snow White and the Seven Dwarfs*《白雪公主》：世界电影史上第一部剧情长篇动画
根据格林童话改编，迪士尼公司 1937 年出品。获得 1938 年第 11 届奥斯
别奖。

12. *Star Wars*　《星球大战》：参见 Chapter13-21。

20. Fred Parke　弗雷德里克·帕克：毕业于美国犹他州大学，1974年获得计算机博士学位，帕克制作了历史上第一个人脸三维计算机模型，该模型在 1976 年《未来世界》一片中使用。帕克现为美国德克萨斯州农工大学(Texas A&M University)建筑学院教授和可视化实验室主任。

21. *Star Wars*　《星球大战》：是美国导演乔治·卢卡斯所制作拍摄的一系列科幻电影。特效公司"工业光魔(ILM)"随影片一齐诞生，成为第一个具有划时代意义的特效电影公司。1977 版《星球大战》被认为开启了特效电影的一个数码科技新时代。

目 录

Part 1
基础篇

Animation English Course

1 CHAPTER

Text

Animation History

Animation is a graphic representation of drawings to show movement within those drawings. A series of drawings are linked together and usually photographed by a camera. The drawings have been slightly changed between individualized **frames**[1] so when they are played back in rapid succession (24 frames per second) there appears to be seamless movement within the drawings.

Pioneers of animation include **Winsor McCay**[2] of the United States and **Emile Cohl**[3] and **Georges Melies**[4] of France. Some consider McCay's ***Sinking of the Lusitania***[5] from 1918 as the first animated feature film.

Early animations, which started appearing before 1910, consisted of simple drawings photographed one at a time. It was extremely labor intensive as there were literally hundreds of drawings per minute of film. The development of **celluloid**[6] around 1913 quickly made animation easier to manage. Instead of numerous drawings, the animator now could make a complex **background** and/or **foreground**[7] and sandwich moving **characters**[8] in between several other pieces of celluloid, which is transparent except for where drawings are painted on it. This made it unnecessary to repeatedly draw the background as it remained static and only the characters moved. It also created an illusion of depth, especially if foreground elements were placed in the frames.

Walt Disney took animation to a new level. He was the first animator to add sound to his movie cartoons with the premiere of ***Steamboat Willie***[9] in 1928. In 1937, he produced the first **full length animated feature film**[10], ***Snow White and the Seven Dwarfs***[11].

With the introduction of computers, animation took on a whole new meaning. Many feature films of today had animation incorporated into them for special effects. A film like ***Star Wars***[12] by **George Lucas**[13] would rely heavily on **computer animation**[14] for many of its special effects. *Toy Story*, produced by **Walt Disney Studios**[15] and Pixar Animation Studios, became the first full length feature film animated entirely on computers when it was released in 1995.

With the advent of personal computers, it has now become possible for the average person to create animations.

Words and Phrases

representation [,reprizen'teiʃən]
n. 再现

in rapid succession ['si:mlis]
紧接地，一连串地

seamless ['si:mlis]
adj. 无缝的；无缝合线的

extremely [ik'stri:mli]
adv. 非常，极其；极端地

literally ['litərəli]
adv. 确实的；真正的

sandwich ['sænwidʒ]
vt. 夹入

in between
在…中间

transparent [træns'pærənt]
adj. 透明的

static ['stætik]
adj. 静态的

illusion [i'lju:ʒən]
n. 幻觉，错觉

element ['elimənt]
n. 元素；要素

premiere [pri'miə, prə'mjer]
v. 初次公演；首次露面

incorporate into
纳入；并入

rely [ri'lai]
vi. 依靠；信赖

entirely [in'taiəli]
adv. 完全地，彻底地

with the advent of
随着…的出现(到来)

Notes

1. **frame** 帧，画面

2. **Winsor McCay** 温瑟 · 麦凯**(1871—1934)**：美国早期动画的开创者，生于美国密歇根州(Michigan)，1914 年推出了一部剧情动画片《恐龙葛蒂》(*Gertie the Dinosaur*)，作品把故事、角色和真人表演等组织成为互动式的情节。继《恐龙葛蒂》之后，温瑟•麦凯又制作了《露斯坦尼亚号之沉没》(*Sinking of the Lusitania*)，是第一部以动画方式制作的纪录片。温瑟 · 麦凯不但是动画情节设计的开创者，也是第一个提出“Full Animation”概念的人，即每秒 24 帧的动画。

3. **Emile Cohl** 埃米尔 · 科尔**(1857—1938)**：出生于法国巴黎，是法国著名动画家，也是世界动画史上的先驱人物，也是个著名漫画家，1908 年制作法国第一部影片《幻影集》(*Fantasmagorie*)，影片运用停格拍摄技术，表现不断变化的图像。

4. **Georges Melies** 乔治 · 梅里爱**(1861—1938)**：默片时代法国著名导演，以在电影特技方面的发明和实践著称，被称为“电影特技之父”，同时也是世界上最早的制片厂创建人。

5. ***Sinking of the Lusitania*** 《露斯坦尼亚号之沉没》：温瑟 · 麦凯(Winsor McCay)1918 年的作品，是第一部以动画方式制作的纪录片。

6. **celluloid** 赛璐珞： 电影胶片材料，1855 年由英国人亚历山大 · 帕克斯(1813—1890)发明，于 1870 年由美国制造公司命名为 Celluloid ，之后赛璐珞逐渐被用于生产照片、胶卷等材料，1913 年左右开始运用在动画制作上。

7. **background/foreground** 动画背景/前景

8. character 角色

9. ***Steamboat Willie***《蒸汽船威利》： 世界第一部有声卡通片，于 1928 年在纽约首映，也是迪士尼第一次向观众介绍米老鼠这一著名动画人物。

10. full length animated feature film 动画电影长片

11. ***Snow White and the Seven Dwarfs***《白雪公主》：世界电影史上第一部剧情长篇动画电影，根据格林童话改编，迪士尼公司 1937 年出品。获得 1938 年第 11 届奥斯卡金像奖特别奖。

12. ***Star Wars*** 《星球大战》：参见 Chapter13-21。

13. George Lucas 乔治 · 卢卡斯：美国的电影导演、制片人和编剧，1944 年生于美国加州，其最著名的作品是《星球大战》(*Star Wars*)和《夺宝奇兵》(*Raiders of the Lost Ark*)系列，作品曾经打破多项票房纪录。2005 年，获得美国电影学会(American Film Institute)颁发的"AFI 终身成就奖"。乔治 · 卢卡斯与弗朗西斯 · 福特 · 科波拉(Francis Ford Coppola)、马丁 · 斯科塞斯(Martin Scorsese)和史蒂文 · 斯皮尔伯格(Steven Spielberg)并称好莱坞 20 世纪 80 年代四大导演。

14. computer animation 电脑动画：参见 Chapter13。

15. Walt Disney Studios 迪士尼工作室：美国著名动画公司，拍摄了世界上第一部剧情长篇动画电影《白雪公主》。华特 · 迪士尼公司(Walt Disney Company) 创立于 1932 年，总部设在美国加州西部城市伯班克(Burbank)，如今旗下掌控四个主要集团公司：迪士尼电影工作室(Walt Disney Studios)、迪士尼乐园(Parks and Resorts)、迪士尼娱乐产品公司(Disney Consumer Products)和媒体与网络公司(Media Networks)。

Comprehensive Questions

1. Why is the application of celluloid a revolution in the history of animation?
2. Why is Walt Disney important?
3. Do you think the heavy reliance on the computer is a good thing? Explain your point.
4. Introduce the history of animation briefly.

Further Reading

◎***Enchanted Drawings: The History of Animation***

Author：Charles Solomon

Publisher：Random House Value Publishing (1994)

◎***Cartoons: One Hundred Years of Cinema Animation***

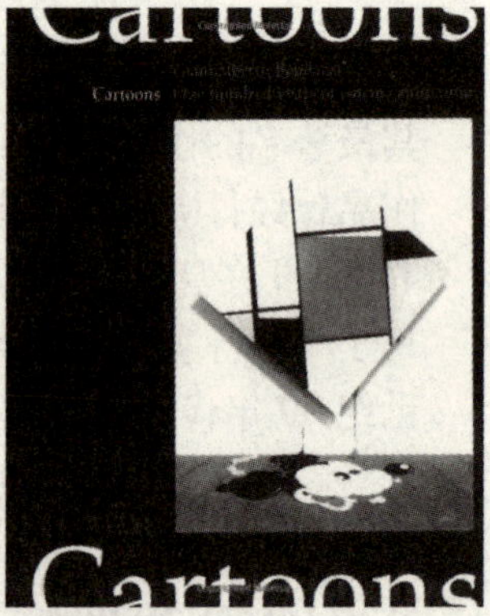

Author：Giannalberto Bendazzi

Publisher：Indiana University Press (1995)

Web Links

www.animationstudies.org

www.goldenagecartoons.com

2 CHAPTER

Text

Beginners(1)

The word Animate comes from the Latin verb animare, which means "to make alive or to fill with breath". We can take our most childlike dreams or the wackiest worlds we can imagine and bring into life. In animation we can completely restructure reality. We take drawings, clay, puppets, or forms on a computer screen, and we make them seem so real that we want to believe they're alive.

Even more than most films, animation is visual. While you're writing, try to keep a movie running inside your head. Visualize what you're writing. Many cartoon writers are also artists, and they begin their thinking by drawing or doodling. The best animation is action, not talking heads. Even though **Hanna-Barbera**[1] was known for its **limited animation**[2], Joseph Barbera used to tell his artists that if he saw six frames of **storyboard**[3] and the characters were still talking, the staff was in trouble. Start the story with action. Animation must be visual!

Time and space are important elements of animation. In animation the audience accepts data quickly. Viewers can register information in just a few frames. **Timing**[4] is very important in animation, just as it is in comedy. The pace of gags is quick. Normally, there are more pages in an animation script than those in a comparable,

live-action[5] script, partially because everything moves so fast.

Animation uses extremes—everything is exaggerated. Comedy is taken to its limits. Jokes that seem impossible in live-action are the best, although with today's **special effects**[6], there is little that can be done in animation that cannot be done in live-action film as well.

The Script[7]

Usually animation begins with a script. If there is no script, then there is at least some kind of idea in written form—an outline or **treatment**[8]. In television a one-page written premise is usually submitted for each **episode**[9]. When a premise is approved, it's expanded into an outline, and the outline is then expanded into a full script. Some **feature films**[10] and some of the shorter television cartoons may have no detailed script. Instead, creation takes place primarily during the storyboard process. Each television series has a **story editor**[11] who is in charge of this process.

Producers[12] and **directors**[13] have approval rights on the finished script. Producer and director are terms with no precise and standard meaning in the United States, and they can be interchangeable or slightly different from studio to studio. Independent producers may deal more with financing and budgets, but producers at the major animation studios may be more directly involved with production.

Recording[14]

About the time the script is finalized, the project is cast. The actors may be given a separate actor's script for recording. Sometimes they get character designs or a storyboard if they are ready in time. A **voice director**[15] will probably direct. Some studios still prefer to record all the actors at once for a television project, as if they were doing a radio play. However, each actor may be recorded separately. This is especially likely if the project is an animated feature. Individual recording sessions make it easier to schedule the actors, work with each actor, move the process along, and fine-tune the timing when it's edited. The directors usually work with a **composer**[16], who may be brought in early for a feature.

The Storyboard

Storyboard artists[17] take the script and create the first visualization of the story. Often these boards are still a little rough. The dialogue and action are listed underneath each frame. Usually, an **animatic**[18] or video of these frames is scanned or filmed from the board when it's complete. This animatic, which includes any recorded sound, helps the director see the episode in the rough and helps in timing the cartoon.

The storyboard process may take about a year for a feature. The script or treatment will undergo many changes as the visual development progresses. Feature storyboard drawings are cleaned up and made into a **flipbook**[19]. Finally the drawings are scanned or **shot**[20], the recorded and available sound is added, and the material is made into a **story reel**[21]. Any necessary changes discovered during the making of the animatic or story reel are made on the storyboard. The building of the story reel is an ongoing process throughout production. Later **breakdowns**[22], then penciled animation, and finally complete animation will be substituted.

Words and Phrases

Animate ['ænimeit, 'ænimət]
n. 动画(绘制)

fill with
装满，充满

wacky ['wæki]
adj. (美国俚语)古怪的，荒诞的

clay [klei]
n. 黏土

puppet ['pʌpit]
n. 木偶

doodle ['du:dl]
v. 涂鸦

action ['ækʃən]
n. 行动；活动；情节

talking heads
电视(或电影)屏幕上发表讲话人的头部特写

pace [peis, 'peisi]
n. 节奏

exaggerated [ig'zædʒəreitid]
adj. 夸张的

outline ['autlain]
n. 大纲；概要

premise [pri'maiz, 'premis]
n. 前提

approve [ə'pru:v]
vt. 批准

in charge of
负责；主管

interchangeable [,intə'tʃeindʒəbl]
adj. 可互换的

financing [fi'nænsiŋ]
n. 融资；筹措资金

budget ['bʌdʒit]
n. 预算

finalize ['fainəlaiz]
vi. 最后定下来；定案

in time
及时

fine-tune ['faintju:n]
vt. 调整；微调

bring in
带来，引进

visualization [,vizjuəlai'zeiʃən]
n. 形象化

rough [rʌf]
adj. 粗糙的

underneath [,ʌndə'ni:θ]
prep. 在…的形式下；在…下面

scan [skæn]
vt. 扫描

in the rough
大致上的；未完成的

undergo [,ʌndə'gəu]
vt. 经历，经受

ongoing ['ɔn, gəuiŋ]
adj. 不间断的；前进的

substitute ['sʌbstitju:t]
vt. 用…代替

Notes

1. **Hanna-Barbera Cartoons, Inc.** 汉纳 · 巴贝拉卡通工作室：20 世纪后半期在北美电视动画领域占主导地位的工作室。1957 年，由威廉姆 · 汉纳(William Hanna 1910—2001)和约瑟夫 · 巴贝拉(Joseph Barbera 1911—2006)创建。两人都是美国好莱坞动画界的传奇人物，创作了著名动画作品《猫和老鼠》(*Tom and Jerry*)，获得多项奥斯卡奖。

2. **limited animation** 低成本动画：在卡通动画制作过程中，整个影片出现的共同影像，可以在画面中重复使用。

3. **storyboard** 分镜头脚本故事板

4. **timing** 时间选择与控制

5. **live action** (和动画电影相对应的)真人与实景电影

6. **special effect** 特效，特技

7. **script** 剧本，脚本

8. **treatment** 影视剧的情节大纲：在前期策划阶段用于陈述导演关于影片纲要的文件。

9. **episode** 一段故事情节或插曲

10. **feature films** 电影长片：通常在影院或电视台播映的完整长度影片。

11. **story editor** 剧本编审

12. **producer** 制片人：制作团队的关键成员，负责确保影片在限定的时间和预算范围内进行制作，并从导演的角度支持项目制作，与投资方和发行商谈判所有的发行及相关事宜。

13. **director** 导演：影视制作团队的领导者，负责把握整部影片的演绎手法、视听风格和动作节奏。

14. **recording** 录音

15. **voice director** 声音导演

16. **composer** 作曲家：负责为影片编写和安排音乐内容的专业人员。

17. **storyboard artist** 故事板艺术家

18. **animatic** 动态故事板：为了让导演和动画师对故事本身进行审查，将故事板按时间分配及顺序对故事板进行动态影像化并制作出样片的过程。动态故事板早期时也被称为莱卡带(Leica reel)。

19. **flipbook** 翻页动画书，手翻书

20. **shot** 镜头：摄像机不间断拍摄的一组帧序列，它常被看成一部视频的最小结构单位。在文中是动词，指拍摄。

21. **story reel** 故事录影带：经过清理的故事板稿本被扫描或拍摄后，将录制好的声音加入其中，制作成为故事录影带，方便导演从整体上把握影片的结构并且有效地控制时间。

22. **breakdown** 受控制帧：是一种特殊的关键帧，它与临近关键帧在时间上保持一定的比例关系。

Comprehensive Questions

1. What did Joe Barbera tell his staff? Why did he say so?
2. In what ways is animation different from live-action film?
3. What are the advantages of individual recording?
4. Tell how the storyboard process is going on.
5. What's the key point to make the best animation?

Further Reading

◎***Animation Unleashed: 100 Principles Every Animator, Comic Book Writers, Filmmakers, Video Artist, and Game Developer Should Know***

Author: Ellen Besen, Illustrator: Bryce Hallett

Publisher: Michael Wiese Productions (2008)

◎***Prepare to Board! Creating Story and Characters for Animated Features and Shorts***

Author: Nancy Beiman

Publisher: Focal Press (2007)

Web Links

www.goldenagecartoons.com

3 CHAPTER

Text

Beginners(2)

Background Design[1]

A **production designer**[2] or background designer is responsible for all location designs. A background painter will paint a few key backgrounds and ship them overseas to be matched by other painters painting additional backgrounds. Very little animation production is done in the United States due to the high costs. In feature production the visual development artists may be working both on story and design at once, making many **concept drawings**[3] before the final designs are chosen and refined for actual production. Background artists usually paint in the traditional way, but some or all elements can be painted digitally.

Color

Color stylists[4], who are supervised by the art director, set the color **palette**[5] for a show. It's important that colors they choose should not only match well but make the characters stand out from the background.

Layout[6]

Layouts are detailed **renderings**[7] of all the storyboard drawings and breakdowns of some of the action between those drawings. They include drawings for each background **underlay, overlay**[8], the start and stop drawings for action of each character, and **visual effects**[9]. Layout artists further refine each shot, setting **camera angles**[10] and **movements**[11], composition, **staging**[12], and lighting. Drawings are made to the proper size and drawn on model. Key layout drawings may be done before a production is shipped overseas, with the remainder done by overseas artists. Layout may also be skipped, basically, if we make detailed drawings at the storyboard stage. Later these can be blown up to the correct size, and elements are separated and used as layouts.

Animation[13]

The animator receives the dialogue track of his section of the story, a storyboard or workbook that has been timed out, the **model sheets**[14], copies of the layouts, and **X-sheets**[15]. There are boxes on the X-sheets for the animator to fill in with the details, layer by layer, as the animation is planned. Animation paper, which is also used by the layout artists and background artists, has a series of holes for pegs so that it can be lined up correctly for a camera. For an **animated feature**[16], animation **pencil tests**[17] may be made prior to principal animation to test the gags and the animation. In television and **direct-to-video**[18] projects, **key animators**[19] may animate the more important action before it is sent overseas for the major animation to be completed.

Clean-up[20] artists or **assistant animators**[21] clean up the rough animation poses drawn by the animator and sketch the key action in between. A breakdown artist or **inbetweener**[22] may be responsible for the easier poses between those. Visual effects animators animate elements like fire, water, and props. For a feature production where drawings are animated, a single minute of film may take over 1,400 drawings. So you see how labor-intensive the animation is!

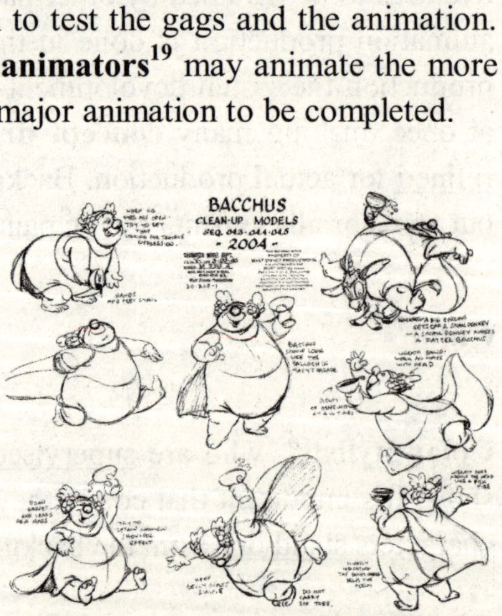

Scene Planning[23]

Scene planners break down all the elements of each scene and check that the scenes are ready for scanning or shipping. A scene planner will set up all the elements in the computer and make sure that they will work correctly. These professionals have excellent technical knowledge. They check all math and verify that each scene and all the camera moves have been set up in the best way. They will also check up whether color effects are set up properly for the painters.

Words and Phrases

due to
由于

refine [ri'fain]
v. 精炼，提纯；改善

supervise ['sju:pəvaiz]
v. 监督，管理；指导

stand out
突出，鲜明

underlay [ˌʌndə'lei]
n. 衬底；支撑物

remainder [ri'meində]
n. 余数；剩余物

blow up
放大

a series of
一连串的；一系列的

prior to
在…前，先于

prop [prɔp]
n. 小道具

labor-intensive [leibəin'tensiv]
adj. 劳动密集型的

break down
分解

verify ['verifai]
vt. 检验；校准

Notes

1. **background design** 动画背景设计：通常以叠层的形式置于动画动作的背后，但有时也会置于之前。

2. **production designer** 美工师

3. **concept drawings** 概念图：将电影场景中的动作进行视觉化的草图方案，可以为团队提供准确思路。

4. **stylist** 样式设计师，造型师

5. **palette** 色板：绘图软件中可以选择颜色的调板。游戏和网络动画中可以使用的颜色通常极为有限。

6. **layout** 设计稿：动画专用名词，在工作性质上接近中文的“构图”，用以展示场景中的所有物体，简单的分为背景设计稿和角色设计稿。背景构图师需要分析某一场景如何运镜取景，以及画面所需的光线和阴影；角色构图师则需要设计并绘制出角色的比例、位置、姿态和动向。设计稿完成后，会根据摄影表(x-sheet)将其再次制作成动态故事板(animatic)，让制作者对作品进行再次审核。

7. **rendering** 效果图，渲染

8. **underlay/overlay** 特指动画的背景和前景

9. **visual effect** 视觉特效

10. **camera angle** 摄影机角度

11. **camera movement** 摄影机运动：指电影摄影机的运动，目的在于跟随一个动作，或改变被摄场景、人物或物体的呈现方式。

12. **staging** 演出布局：参见 Chapter5-7。

13. **animation** 动画：动画制作的核心阶段，即具体的拍摄阶段，是在由设计稿(layout)制作的动态故事板(animatic)通过后进行。

14. **model sheet** 角色设计：一般角色设计图分服饰设计图、脸部表情设计图和局部装饰设计图，经常从正面、侧面、背面等不同的角度进行表现。有时为了能更好的观察和绘制，部分角色或是物品将被雕塑成实体的模型。在角色设计进行的同时，美术指导(art directors)和色彩设计师(color stylists)将一起决定作品的艺术风格以及色彩使用方案。

15. **X-sheet(exposure sheet)** 摄影表：它是导演对脚本上每一个镜头所做的指示，它是原画设计动作的参照，也是最后剪辑、合成的依据。

16. animated feature 动画长片

17. pencil test 线拍：在制作场景动画时，原画师(animator)通常会对该场景中的动画进行一次铅笔稿的试拍，线拍是一个动画场景最终形态的初期形式，用来测试该场景中动画的流畅程度。动画师通过线拍来对自己的工作进行审查并做出相应的修改，然后将完善工作交给助理动画师(assistant animators)来添加细节或补充遗漏的帧。

18. direct-to-video 音像版，录像带首映

19. key animator 关键帧画师：在一些成本较高的动画作品中，主要角色的动画将会由动画师组成的专门小组来完成。小组由动画监制(supervising animator)、主动画师(lead animators)和助理动画师(assistant animators)组成。

20. clean-up 清稿：是手绘动画制作流程中的一个部分，主要对通过铅笔稿审查的动画进行清理和重新临摹，使画面更为统一，让整部作品的角色和场景在最终放映时给人有如出自一人之手绘制的感觉。

21. assistant animator 助理动画师：在主动画师(lead animator)的带领下进行关键帧的绘制。

22. inbetweener 中间画画师

23. scene planning 场景规划，场面调度：其概念源自于法语“mise-en-scine”(舞台上的步位)，指在剧场的舞台上一切视觉元素的安排。由于电影和戏剧在艺术处理上具有某些共同性，场面调度一词也被引用到电影创作中。在拍摄过程中电影导演将人与物按照三维空间观念安排，但经过摄像机后，即将实物转换成二维空间的影像，成为景框(frame)中的平面景象。场面调度观念颇为复杂，混合了剧场和平面艺术的视觉传统。

Comprehensive Questions

1. What are layouts?
2. How many kinds of layouts are discussed in the text?
3. What roles do key animators, clean-up animators and visual effects animators play respectively?
4. Why is animation labor-intensive?
5. Explain the work of a scene planner.

Further Reading

◎ ***Animation from Pencils to Pixels: Classical Techniques for the Digital Animator***

Author：Tony White

Publisher: Focal Press (2006)

◎ ***Beginner's Guide to Animation: Everything You Need to Know to Get Started***

Author: Mary Murphy

Publisher: Watson-Guptill (2008)

Web Links

www.disneyanimation.com

4 CHAPTER

Text

Basic Animation Writing Structure

Structure exists to help you write a better story, but differences in the length of your story make a difference in the complexity of your structure. Differences in type(feature, kids'cartoon, Internet short)or **genre**[1] (action/adventure, comedy, preschool) can also make a difference in complexity and style. A feature **script**[2] is longer and requires more structure to hold our interest. An Internet short or one-minute TV cartoon requires very little plot. In fact, structure may get in the way of the **gags**[3]. Generally action/adventure shows require more plot than gag-driven comedy shows. Prime-time animated shows generally use a **sitcom**[4] structure with more clever dialogue and less action.

Basic Structure

All stories must have a beginning, development, climax and end. A short series script(for TV or the Internet)must be about the stars of that series and be centered on them. The star or hero of each episode must have a goal or motive, and someone or something must oppose to that goal. These are the basic story musts, which are applied to a film, too. Of course, there are also independent animated films that are more abstract and make no attempt at telling a tale.

Normally scripts use a **three-act structure**[5]:

- *Act I* This ends after the problem has been set up.(The girl is on top of a flagpole.)

- *Act II* This ends before the **climax**[6].(Someone is pelting her with squishy tomatoes and rotten oranges.)

- *Act III* **Resolution**[7].(She finds a way to get down.)Wrap up with a **tag**[8].

Occasionally a TV animation script will be written in just two acts, but even with only two acts, the basic three-act structure will be spread out over the length of those two acts. The three acts of a typical television script may be about the same length, although the last act will probably be the shortest. Sometimes the first act is shorter. Television act breaks normally come at **commercial**[9] breaks, so suspense should be built up to help keep the audience in their seats through the commercials. There may be an opening teaser.

A three-act feature script will probably have acts that are apportioned: 25 percent for Act I,50 percent for Act II, and 25 percent for Act III. The rules are not carved in stone.

Story Theme[10]

The theme is the lesson that the **protagonist**[11] learns, the central message and values of the story. We just touch briefly on theme when we talk about what the main character learns about himself. Not all animation stories have themes, but many of the best stories do. A theme is something for the audience to think about later. It gives the story some substance. It helps us understand each other and the world around us. It's an observation about life and the people in the world. It helps us to identify with the characters. We recognize our own problems and root for the character to work through those problems, flaws, and needs in order to survive and grow.

Think of a theme as one value coming into **conflict**[12] with another and winning out. Forgiveness is better than revenge. Living for the present can make life fuller than constantly worrying about the future. Pestering your older brother is more fun than playing by yourself...at least until you get caught. These are the basic everyday values of life, and they have been the subjects of stories from the beginning of time. Oral tales of the old; myths; legend; Greek, Roman, and Shakespearean plays; novels; films; and even games have all been centered around these conflicts in values.

Remember your audience. Because male teens are the biggest ticket buyers, many films center on the theme of childishness losing out to adulthood.If your audience are primarily children, then you may want to consider it is appropriate. Universal and timeless themes that touch us all are usually the best themes for films.

Character, plot, and theme are all connected. Your hero may have a character flaw that is getting in the way of his happiness. What he goes through during the course of the story changes the way he treats life and alters the way he'll live in the future. That's his **character arc**[13]. Ideally, he will become a better person, or at least come to know himself and the world much better. Will reaching his goal make life better for your hero and for others? Will the values of the hero or the values of the villain win out, and why? It's possible to have more than one theme, but if this is the case, the themes must be interrelated.

A theme is felt, not indoctrinated or preached. No one wants a sermon. Instead we want characters to show by their actions what they value in life and how they fight for good in the world. Values are expressed mostly through action, but they might come out briefly during the course of a verbal conflict as well. Conflict and opposing values are the heart of any story.

Words and Phrases

structure ['strʌktʃə]
n. 结构

complexity [kəm'pleksiti]
n. 复杂，复杂性；复杂错综的事物

plot [plɔt]
n. 情节

comedy ['kɔmidi]
n. 喜剧

prime-time ['praim'taim]
n. 黄金时段

episode ['episəud]
n. 插曲；情节

motive ['məutiv]
n. 动机，目的

oppose [ə'pəuz]
v. 反对；对抗

apply to
适用于；应用于

attempt at
企图，努力；尝试

flagpole ['flægpəul]
n. 旗杆

pelt [pelt]
vt. 攻击；投掷

squishy ['skwiʃi]
adj. 湿软的

rotten ['rɔtən]
adj. 腐烂的

wrap up
使圆满结束；胜利完成

occasionally [ə'keiʒənəli]
adv. 偶尔，间或

spread out
展开；铺开

typical ['tipikəl]
adj. 典型的；代表性的

come at
达到；接近

suspense [sə'spens]
n. 悬念

teaser ['ti:zə]
n. 引人好奇的广告

apportion [ə'pɔ:ʃən]
vt. 按比例分配

values ['væljuz]
n. 价值观念；价值标准

substance ['sʌbstəns]
n. 要义；本质

observation [,ɔbzə:'veiʃən]
n. 知识，经验

identify with
跟…产生共鸣；与一致

root for
支持；鼓励

work through
解决；完成

flaw [flɔ:]
n. 瑕疵；缺点

in order to
为了，以便；想要

win out
取得胜利；摆脱困境

forgiveness [fə'givnis]
n. 宽恕；宽仁之心

revenge [ri'vendʒ]
n. 报复；复仇

pester ['pestə]
v. 纠缠，烦扰

get caught
被抓住；遭逮捕

oral tales
口头传说

lose out to
输给；被…所取代

go through
经受

villain ['vilən]
n. 坏人；戏剧、小说中的反派角色

interrelated [ˌintəri'leitid]
adj. 相关的；互相联系的

indoctrinate [in'dɔktrineit]
v. 灌输；教导

preach [pri:tʃ]
v. 说教

sermon ['sə:mən]
n. 布道；训诫

fight for
为…而战，而奋斗

verbal conflict
唇舌战，语言交锋

Notes

1. **genre** 艺术作品的类型、风格或流派

2. **script** 脚本：通常记载台词、对话和动作等信息，是使故事脚本或小说详细化的工作，可具体到人物的对话、场景的切换、时间的分割等等。

3. **gag** 笑料：动画中主要依靠人物的形象、夸张的表情、肢体动作等来制造笑料。

4. **sitcom(situation comedy)** 情景喜剧：是出现在广播、电视中的一种喜剧演出形式，一般有固定的主演阵容，一条或多条故事线，围绕着一个或多个固定场景进行。情景喜剧是最受欢迎的电视节目之一。

5. **three-act structure** 三幕结构：指的是剧本的结构，包括开端、中段和结尾三部分。第一幕是开端，即确定故事的主要人物、故事的前提以及故事的情境等，以便及时地抓住观众；第二幕是故事的主体部分，也称为电影剧本的对抗部分，即为故事中的人物规定出需求、目的，然后为这一需求设置障碍，以便能产生故事冲突； 第三幕通常是故事的结局。

6. **climax** 故事发展到最后的高潮阶段

7. **resolution** 故事的结局，尾声

8. **tag** 在剧本或影视剧中起画龙点睛作用的结尾

9. **commercial** 商业广告

10. **theme** 故事的主题：动画中所表达出的价值观，如宽恕、复仇、友谊、环保等主题。

11. **protagonist** 推动故事往前发展的主要角色：这一术语常与明星、英雄交换使用。严格意义上讲，在所有故事中，主角并不总是英雄，英雄也并不总是主角。尤其在神话中，故事的催化剂往往是由反派角色而不是主要角色来承担。

12. **conflict** 冲突：是一切剧作的基础，为人物规定出需求，即在剧本中确立他想要达到什么目的后，就可以为这一目标的实现设置障碍，这样就产生了冲突。

13. **character arc** 角色性格曲线：体现为在故事变化过程中，角色人物最终克服各种局限，使得情境发生改变。

Comprehensive Questions

1. What is the basic structure of a film?
2. Explain the three-act structure.
3. How do you understand the story theme?
4. What is the character arc?

Further Reading

◎ ***Basics Animation: Scriptwriting***

Author: Paul Wells

Publisher: AVA Publishing (2007)

◎***How to Write for Animation***

Author: Jeffrey Scott

Publisher: Overlook TP (2003)

Web Links

www.animation-writer.com

5 CHAPTER

Text

Twelve Basic Principles of Animation (1)

The **12 basic principles of animation**[1] are a set of principles of animation introduced by the Disney animators **Ollie Johnston**[2] and **Frank Thomas**[3] in their book ***The Illusion of Life: Disney Animation***[4](1981). Johnston and Thomas in turn based their book on the work of the leading Disney animators from the 1930s onwards, and their effort to produce more realistic animations. The main purpose of the principles was to produce an illusion of characters adhering to the basic laws of physics, but they also dealt with more abstract issues, such as emotional timing and character appeal.

The book and its principles have become generally adopted, and been referred to as the "Bible of the industry."In 1999 the book was voted number one of the "best animation books of all time" via an online poll. Though the original intention was to apply them to traditional, hand-drawn animation, the principles still have great relevance for today's more prevalent computer animation.

Squash and stretch[5]

The most important principle is "squash and stretch", the purpose of which is to give a sense of weight and flexibility to drawn objects. It can be applied to simple objects, like a bouncing ball, or more complex constructions, like the musculature of a human face. Taken to an extreme point, a figure stretched or squashed to an exaggerated degree can have a comical effect. In realistic animation, however, the most important aspect of this principle is the fact that an object's volume does not change when squashed or stretched. If the length of a ball is stretched vertically, its width (in three dimensions, also its depth) needs to contract correspondingly horizontally.

Anticipation[6]

Anticipation is used to prepare the audience for an action, and to make the action appear more realistic. A dancer jumping off the floor has to bend his knees first; a golfer making a swing has to swing the club back first. The technique can also be used for less physical actions, such as a character looking off-screen to anticipate someone's arrival, or attention focusing on an object that a character is about to pick up. For special effect, anticipation can also be omitted in cases where it is expected. The resulting sense of anticlimax will produce a feeling of surprise in the viewer, and can often add comedy to a scene. This is often referred to as a 'surprise gag'.

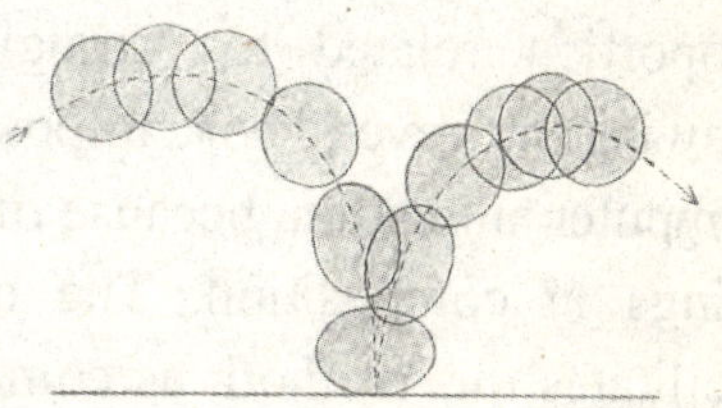

Staging[7]

This principle is akin to staging as it is known in theatre and film. Its purpose is to direct the audience's attention, and make it clear what is of greatest importance in a scene; what is happening, and what is about to happen. Johnston and Thomas defined it as "the presentation of any idea so that it is completely and unmistakably clear", whether that idea is an action, a personality, an expression or a mood. This can be done by various means, such as the placement of a character in the frame, the use of light and shadow, and the angle and position of the camera. The essence of this principle is keeping focus on what is relevant, and avoiding unnecessary detail.

Straight ahead action and pose to pose[8]

These are two different approaches to the actual drawing process. "Straight ahead action" means drawing out a scene frame by frame from beginning to end, while "pose to pose" involves starting with drawing a few, key frames, and then filling in the intervals later. "Straight ahead action" creates a more fluid, dynamic illusion of movement, and is better for producing realistic action sequences. On the other hand, it is hard to maintain proportions, and to create exact, convincing poses along the way. "Pose to pose" works better for dramatic or emotional scenes. A combination of the two techniques is often used.

Computer animation removes the problems of proportion related to "straight ahead action" drawing; however, "pose to pose" is still used for computer animation, because of the advantages it brings in composition. The use of computers facilitates this method, as computers can fill the missing sequences in between poses automatically. It is, however, still important to oversee this process, and apply the other principles discussed.

Words and Phrases

onward ['ɔnwəd]
adv. 向前；在前面

adhere to
遵守；坚持

appeal [ə'pi:l]
n. 吸引力，感染力

referred to as
被称为…

poll [pəul]
n. 民意测验

relevance ['relivəns]
n. 关联

flexibility [ˌfleksi'biliti]
n. 灵活性；弹性

bouncing ['baunsiŋ]
adj. 有弹性的；跳跃的；充满活力的

musculature ['mʌskjulətʃə]
n. 肌肉组织

stretch [stretʃ]
v. 伸展；张开

squash [skwɔʃ, skwɔ:ʃ]
v. 挤压

exaggerated [ig'zædʒəreitid]
adj. 夸张的

vertically ['və:tikəli]
adv. 垂直地

jump off
跳离；出发；开始

club [klʌb]
n. 棍棒

off-screen
银幕外；幕后

anticlimax [,ænti'klaimæks]
突降法，指说话或写作中从有重大意义的精彩内容突然转入平淡的内容，这里是指打破“动画预期”规律的情况。

be akin to
与…同类的；近似的

unmistakably [,ʌnmə'steikəbli]
adv. 明白地

relevant ['reləvənt]
adj. 有重大意义的

prevalent ['prevələnt]
adj. 流行的；普遍的，广传的

dynamic [dai'næmik]
adj. 动态的有活力的

proportion [prəu'pɔ:ʃən]
n. 比例；大小

convince [kən'vins]
vt. 使确信

a combination of
结合；综合

facilitate [fə'siliteit]
vt. 促进，推进，助长

sequence ['si:kwəns]
n. 序列；关联；续发事件

oversee [,əuvə'si:]
vt. 监督，管理

Notes

1. **12 basic principles of animation** 动画的 12 条黄金法则：是由 Disney 的动画师累积数十年的经验所整理出来的指导动画制作的 12 条基本原理。这十二条法则渐渐成为手绘卡通角色动画的基础之一，并影响到三维动画创作领域。

2. **Ollie Johnston** 欧利 · 约翰斯顿(1912—2008)：迪士尼九大元老之一，是很多迪士尼重量级角色的创作者，作品有《幻想曲》、《小鹿斑比》、《小飞侠》、《睡美人》、《森林王子》等。

3. **Frank Thomas** 弗兰克 · 托马斯(1912—2004)：迪士尼九大元老之一，他创造了很多迪士尼动画中经典而感人的场景，作品有《白雪公主》、《小鹿斑比》、《小姐与流浪汉》等。

4. ***The Illusion of Life: Disney Animation*** 《迪士尼——生命的景象》：弗兰克 · 托马斯(Frank Thomas)和欧利 · 约翰斯顿(Ollie Johnston)所著，颇具影响的经典动画著作。

5. **Squash and stretch** 压缩与伸展：物体受到力的挤压，产生拉长或者压扁的变形状况，再加上夸张的表现方式，使得物体本身看起来有弹性、有质量、富有生命力，因此较容易产生戏剧性。

6. **Anticipation** 预备动作、动画预期：让观众能够产生“预期性”或者让观众预知角色的下一步动作。

7. **Staging** 演出布局：在动画中的构图、运镜、动作、走位都需要仔细的设计安排，避免在同一时间又过多琐碎的动作与变化。精心设计好每一个镜头与动作，不仅可以加强动画的整体感，也可以省去许多不必要的成本浪费。

8. **Straight ahead action and pose to pose** 连续运动与姿态对应：两种动作动画的绘制技巧。连续动作是将动作从第一张开始，依照顺序画到最后一张，通常是制作较简易的动态；姿势对应，是将动作拆解成一些重要的定格动作，补上中间的间补动画后，产生动态的效果，通常适用于较复杂的动作。

Comprehensive Questions

1. Give your examples to illustrate the 4 principles discussed in this chapter.
2. What are the advantages of the "pose to pose"principle in computer animation?

Further Reading

◎ ***Walt Disney's Nine Old Men and the Art of Animation***

Author: John Canemaker

Publisher: Disney Editions (2001)

Web Links

www.animationarena.com

6 CHAPTER

Text

Twelve Basic Principles of Animation (2)

Follow through and overlapping action[1]

"Follow through" means that separate parts of a body will continue moving after the character has stopped. "Overlapping action" is the tendency for parts of the body to move at different rates. Again, use of the technique can produce a comical effect, while more realistic animation must time the actions exactly, to produce a convincing result.

Slow in and slow out[2]

The movement of the human body, and most other objects, needs time to accelerate and slow down. For this reason, an animation looks more realistic if it has more frames near the beginning and end of a movement, and fewer in the middle. This principle goes for characters moving between two extreme poses, such as sitting down and standing up, but also for inanimate, moving objects, like the bouncing ball in the above illustration.

Arcs[3]

Most human and animal actions occur along an arched trajectory, and animation should reproduce these movements for greater realism. This can apply to a limb moving by rotating a joint, or a thrown object moving along a parabolic trajectory. The exception is mechanical movement, which typically moves in straight lines.

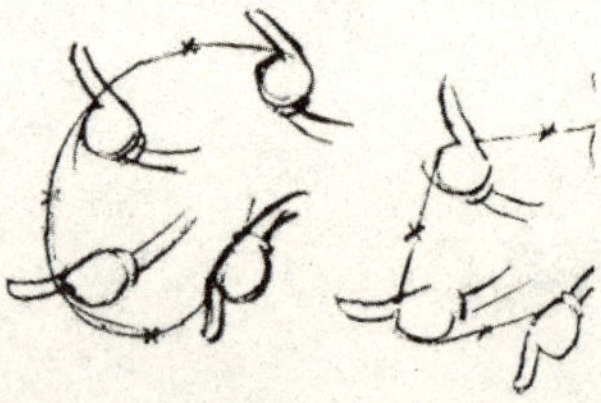

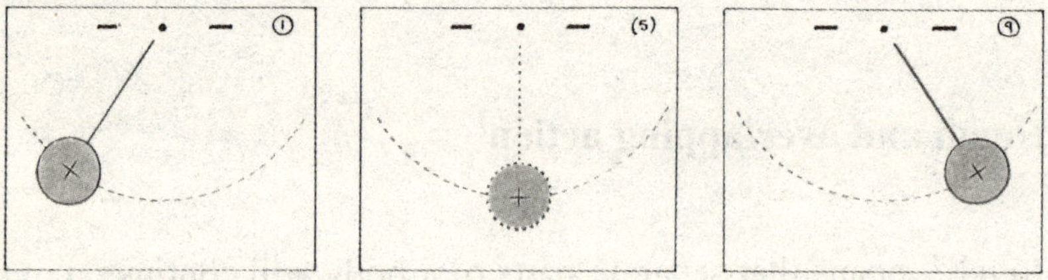

Secondary action[4]

Adding secondary actions to the main action gives a scene more life, and can help to support the main action. A person walking can simultaneously swing his arms or keep them in his pockets, he can speak or whistle, or he can express emotions through facial expressions. The important thing about secondary actions is that they emphasize, rather than take attention away from the main action. If the latter is the case, those actions are better left out.

Timing and Weight[5]

Timing in reality refers to two different concepts: physical timing and theatrical timing. It is essential both to the physical realism, as well as to the storytelling of the animation, that the timing is right. On a purely physical level, correct timing makes objects appear to abide to the laws of physics; for instance, an object's weight decides how it reacts to an impetus, like a push. Theatrical timing is of a less technical nature, and is developed mostly through experience. It can be pure comic timing, or it can be used to convey deep emotions. It can also be a device to communicate aspects of a character's personality.

Exaggeration[6]

Exaggeration is an effect especially useful for animation, as perfect imitation of reality can look static and dull in cartoons. The level of exaggeration depends on whether one seeks realism or a particular style, like a caricature or the style of an artist. Other forms of exaggeration can involve the supernatural or surreal, alterations in the physical features of a character, or elements in the storyline itself. It is important to employ a certain level of restraint when using exaggeration; if a scene contains several elements, there should be a balance in how those elements are exaggerated in relation to each other, to avoid confusing or overawing the viewer.

Solid drawing[7]

The principle of solid — or good — drawing, really means that the same principles apply to an animator as to an academic artist. The animator needs to be a skilled **draughtsman**[8] and has to understand the basics of anatomy, composition, weight, balance, light and shadow etc. For the classical animator, this involved taking art classes and doing sketches from life. One thing in particular that Johnston and Thomas warned against was creating "twins": characters whose left and right sides mirrored each other, and looked lifeless. Modern-day computer animators in theory do not need to draw at all, yet their work can still benefit greatly from a basic understanding of these principles.

Appeal[9]

A character who is appealing is not necessarily sympathetic — villains or monsters can also be appealing — the important thing is that the viewer feels the character is real and interesting. There are several tricks for making a character connect better with the audience; for likable characters a symmetrical or particularly baby-like face tends to be effective.

Words and Phrases

convincing [kən'vinsiŋ]
adj. 令人信服的；有说服力的

trajectory ['trædʒiktəri]
n. 轨道

rotate [rəu'teit]
v. 旋转；转动

parabolic [ˌpærə'bɔlik]
adj. 抛物线状的

simultaneously [saiməl'teiniəsli]
adv. 同时地

left out
忽视，不考虑

abide to
vt. 接受；遵守

impetus ['impitəs]
n. 动量，动力

convey [kən'vei]
vt. 传送，传递

device [di'vais]
n. 手法，技巧

static ['stætik]
adj. 不活泼的；缺乏活力的

dull [dʌl]
adj. 枯燥无味的

caricature ['kærikətjuə]
n. 漫画；讽刺画；漫画手法

restraint [ri'streint]
n. 约束力

overawe [ˌauvə'rɔ:]
vt. 威慑；吓住；使大感敬畏

anatomy [ə'nætəmi]
n. 解剖学；形态学

warned against
警告…不要；提醒…提防

trick [trik]
n. 诀窍；秘诀

symmetrical [si'metrikəl]
adj. (身材等)匀称的；整齐的

Notes

1. **Follow through and overlapping action** 跟随与重叠动作：跟随动作，是将物体的各部位拆解，通常是没有骨架的部位较容易产生跟随的动作，例如动物的尾巴，头发，衣服的末梢等等。重叠动作，是将移动中物体的各部位拆解，将其动作的时间错开，产生分离重叠的时间差与夸张的变形，增加动画戏剧性与表现力，达到更容易吸引观众的目的，也强化了动画的趣味。

2. **Slow in and slow out** 慢进与慢出：一般动作在开始与结束时速度较慢，中间过程速度较快一些，因为一般动作并非等速度运动，这是正常的物理现象。静止的物体开始移动时由慢而快，而将要停止时的物体则会由快变慢，若以等速度方式开始或者结束动作，则会产生一种唐突的感觉。

3. **Arcs** 弧形运动：动画中的动作，基本上除了机械的动作之外，几乎所有的动线都是以抛物线的方式进行，所以在绘制动线时，非机械式的物体，移动时不要完全以直线的方式运行，而机械式的物体，则使用较僵硬的直线运动，这样可以较容易的区别机械与非机械物体的属性，也可强化这两种完全不同的物体的个性。

4. **Secondary action** 第二动作：依附在主要动作之下的细微动作，虽然是属于比较微小的动作，但实际上却有画龙点睛的效果。第二动作并非不重要的动作，而是强化主要动作的关键，不仅可以使角色更生动真实，更可让角色感觉有生命。

5. **Timing and Weight** 时间节奏与量感：动画的灵魂就是物体与角色的运动，而控制运动的关键就是动作的节奏与重量感。动作的节奏就是速度的快慢，过快或者过慢都会让该动作看起来不自然，而不同的角色也会有不用的节奏，因为动作的节奏会影响到角色的个性，也会影响到动作自然与否；另一个控制运动的关键就是指量感，因为所有的物体都是有质量的，而节奏可以表现物体的质量，这和一般人对自然界的认知有关。

6. **Exaggeration** 夸张：动画通常运用夸张的角色表演来强化剧情的起伏，让观众更容易融入剧情并且乐在其中。夸张不是只把动作幅度扩大而已，而是巧妙且适当地将剧情所需要的情绪释放出来。动画师在诠释角色时对夸张程度的把握，都是动画精彩与否的关键。

7. **Solid drawing** 扎实的描绘：动画的制作，视觉表现占了很大一部分，而视觉表现则需要非常扎实的绘画训练以及对美感的敏锐感知度，不论是制作传统动画或者是电脑动画都一样，动画师都需要有扎实的绘画基础训练，才能将动画中所需要的画面完整的表现出来。

8. **daughtsman** 擅长于描绘的美术家

9. **Appeal** 吸引力：吸引力是任何一种艺术都要具备的条件，动画通常最吸引人的地方，就是充满想象力的画面表达。

Comprehensive Questions

1. Pick out 4 principles from those discussed in this chapter and give your examples to illustrate them.
2. How is physical timing different from theatrical timing?
3. Of all the principles discussed in the two chapters,which do you think is the most interesting in animation? Explain why.

Further Reading

◎ ***The Illusion of Life: Disney Animation***

Author: Ollie Johnston

Publisher: Disney Editions; Rev Sub edition (1995)

Web Links

www.disneyanimation.com

Part 2

人物篇

Animation English Course

7 CHAPTER

Text

Ponyo, or Hayao Miyazaki's Inner Child

A contemporary magician, an authentic poet marrying the most unique ideas to the most oniric images, director **Hayao Miyazaki**[1] is back to offer us one of his most touching fables, ***Ponyo***[2], released in theaters recently.

Four years after ***Howl's Moving Castle***[3], this Japanese master chose to produce his latest animation wonder all by hand, without computers, in a plain **visual style**[4]**,** which gives his characters and backgrounds a familiar aspect and an energy that can be achieved only in **traditional animation**[5]. His vision of the film being born as he was staring at the ocean during a storm, he gave a particular attention to the rendering of the sea and of the waves, creating a world far beyond our expectations. But, above all, he proposes a magnificent poem on childhood…

Interview

Animated Views: How would you describe your latest film?

Hayao Miyazaki: It is the story of Ponyo, a little fish-girl who dreams to be with **Sosuke**[6], a five-year old boy who promised to take care of her. It is also about how Sosuke keeps his promise. *Ponyo* is a love story between two young children and it's at the same time a wonderful adventure: an adaptation of **Hans Christian Andersen**'s[7] ***The Little Mermaid***[8] in present-day Japan.

A small town near the sea, a house at the top of a cliff, a few characters and the ocean, seen as a presence, a living entity. A world where magic and alchemy are part of everyday life. Down, like our unconscious mind, the deep sea, and at the surface, the tumult of the waves. As to the change of space and shapes, the sea becomes not only the setting of our story, but one of the main **protagonists**[9]. A small boy and a little girl, love and responsibility, ocean and life, and the essence of all is: Ponyo -- a fairytale tells us the answer to the distress and uncertainty of our times.

AV: The first **draft**[10] of your story seemed to rather lean toward the relationship between a mother and her son.

HM: When I'm working on a project, I write ideas down and then I change lots of things. What I write at first is always different from the final film. My first idea was to depict a character, at the beginning of her life, searching deep within herself, including her relation ship with her child. I figured out Sosuke's mother was 25 years old, but my collaborators thought she was too young. They realized she was even younger than themselves. They felt it difficult in drawing a mother who was less than 35. My team has grown older…

AV: In the end, the subject of your film is childhood itself, through the eyes of that extraordinary child Sosuke.

HM: I wanted Sosuke and Ponyo to act naturally. Many **scenes**[11] were acted according to their desires. When Ponyo splashes Sosuke, he's not frightened. If he were, they wouldn't become friends. Sosuke is the only one who is not bothered by that. General speaking, children aren't glad to be treated like that, but he doesn't care. As you're watching the film, you're not surprised at his reaction, he's truly believable. And when Ponyo turns back into a fish thanks to her magical power, he's not impressed.

He just says she's great. He's a funny little guy. During the **dubbing**[12] session, people really liked his reaction. Sosuke truly admires Ponyo. He doesn't ask any question. He accepts everything, and that's wonderful. Then you wonder what is going to happen to him. He accepts everything but, to me, it won't be everlasting.

AV: The movie is much about children's promises, as Sosuke promises to take care of Ponyo.

HM: That's the point, but one doesn't always keep true to one's word. It's like a baby chicken that you want to protect but finally it dies despite your care. Today, when you grow older, you have to learn not to keep your promises. That's to said, in my movie, I want to show such a child's behavior.

AV: You mean, things change when you grow up.

HM: I imagine, if Ponyo went to the Kindergarten, she would get closer to Kumilo and would leave Sosuke…

AV: How sad!

HM: Not at really. It may be a relief for Sosuke, or not. But I think things are not that simple for him. You can imagine Sosuke should marry Ponyo, but life is not that simple.

AV: Dealing with childhood, you're handling something essential, something that is related to our origins. Hence the scene for the young parents.

HM: It had to be. It's difficult for Ponyo to fit in. I wanted to present her a man who grows up and evolves a lot. Her faculties allow her to succeed. It's strength. In that scene, she really cares, and she can communicate with the baby, but not with words. I consider it a means of communication anterior to humans.

Introduction

Hayao Miyazaki (born on January 5, 1941) is a prominent Japanese **filmmaker**[13] of many popular **animated feature films**[14]. He is also a co-founder of **Studio Ghibli**[15], an animation studio and production company.

He remained unknown to the West, until **Miramax**[16] released his 1997 **Princess Mononoke**[17]. By that time, his films had already enjoyed both commercial and critical success in Japan. Princess Mononoke was the highest-grossing film in Japan until **Titanic**[18] (1997) came out a few months later, and the first animated film to win Picture of the Year at the **Japanese Academy Awards**[19]. His later film, **Spirited Away**[20], had that distinction as well, and was the first anime film to win an **Academy Award**[21], topping Titanic in the Japanese **box office**[22]. Howl's Moving Castle was also nominated, but did not receive the award.

Miyazaki's films often incorporate recurrent themes, such as human beings' relationship with nature and technology, and the difficulty of maintaining a pacifist ethic. Reflecting Miyazaki's feminism, the protagonists of his films are often strong, independent girls or young women; with the exceptions of The **Castle of Cagliostro**[23] and **Castle in the Sky**[24], his films often depict villains to be morally ambiguous characters with redeeming qualities.

Miyazaki's films have generally been financially successful, and this success has invited comparisons with American animator Walt Disney. In 2006, **Time**[25] Magazine voted Miyazaki one of the most influential Asians of the past 60 years.

Words and Phrases

magician [mə'dʒiʃən]
n. 魔术师，变戏法的人

authentic [ɔ:'θentik]
adj. 真正的，名副其实的

touching ['tʌtʃiŋ]
adj. 动人的

wonder ['wʌndə]
n. 奇迹，奇观；美好的事

stare at
凝视，盯住

rendering ['rendəriŋ]
n. 表现；描写

magnificent [mæg'nifisənt]
adj. 壮丽的；宏伟的

adaptation [,ædæp'teʃən]
n. 改编；改编本，改写本

cliff [klif]
n. (海边的)悬崖，峭壁

entity ['entəti]
n. 实体；存在；本质

alchemy ['ælkimi]
n. 魔力

unconscious mind
潜意识；无意识

tumult ['tju:mʌlt]
n. 喧嚣；波动

essence ['esəns]
n. 本质，实质

fairytale ['feəriteil]
n. 童话

distress [di'stres]
n. 危难，不幸；悲痛

lean toward
偏爱

depict [di'pikt]
vt. 描述；描画

collaborator [kə'læbəreitə(r)]
n. 合作者；协作者

extraordinary [ik'strɔ:dənəri]
adj. 非凡的；特别的

splash [splæʃ]
v. 溅，泼

admire [əd'maiə]
vt. 钦佩；赞赏，欣赏

despite [di'spait]
prep. 不管，不顾；尽管，任凭

relief [ri'li:f]
n. 安慰；救济

hence [hens]
adv. 因此；今后

evolve [i'vɔlv]
v. 进化，进展

faculty ['fækəlti]
n. 能力，才能

anterior to
在…之前

nominate ['nɔmineit]
v. 提名

incorporate [in'kɔ:pəreit, in'kɔ:pərət]
vt. 包含；吸收；加入

recurrent [ri'kʌrənt]
adj. 复发的；周期性的，经常发生的

ethic ['eθik]
n. 伦理；道德规范

feminism ['feminizəm]
n. 女权主义；男女平等主义

redeeming [ri'di:miŋ]
adj. 补偿的；弥补的

influential [,influ'enʃəl]
adj. 有影响的；有势力的

Notes

1. **Hayao Miyazaki** 宫崎骏：日本著名动画艺术家，吉卜力工作室(STUDIO GHIBLI)董事。1941 年生于东京都，1963 年以动画师身份进入东映动画公司。1968 年，由东映动画制作的《太阳王子——荷鲁斯大冒险》上映，宫崎骏任原画和场景镜头设计，随后开始逐步担负更重要的工作。 1979 年，宫崎骏首部执导的电影动画作品《鲁邦三世——卡里奥斯特罗之城》问世，其后在知名动画杂志 *Animage* 上连载漫画作品《风之谷》，并于 1984 年执导了该作的电影版，取得了巨大成功。1985 年吉卜力(GHIBLI)工作室成立后制作了多部深受好评的动画电影。

2. ***Ponyo***《悬崖上的金鱼公主》：吉卜力工作室 2008 年推出的动画电影，由宫崎骏编剧并担任导演。作品入围 2008 年第 65 届威尼斯国际电影节(Venice International Film Festival)；获得 2009 年东京动画奖(Tokyo Anime Awards)年度最佳动画和第 32 届日本学院奖(Japan Academy Prize)年度最佳动画。官方网址： www.ghibli.jp/pony。

3. ***Howl's Moving Castle*** 《哈尔的移动城堡》：吉卜力工作室于 2004 年推出的动画电影，宫崎骏导演。作品荣获 2005 年第 62 届威尼斯电影节荣誉银狮奖，2006 年获奥斯卡最佳动画长片奖。

4. **visual style** 视觉风格

5. **traditional animation** 传统动画：传统动画有着一系列的制作工序，它首先要将动画镜头中每一个动作的关键及转折部分先设计出来，也就是要先画出原画，根据原画再画出中间画，即动画，最后经过一张张地描线、上色，逐帧拍摄录制。动画是利用人眼的视觉暂留现象，将一张张逐渐变化的并能清楚地反映一个连续动态过程的静止画面，经过摄像机逐张逐帧地拍摄编辑，使之在屏幕上活动起来。

6. **Sosuke** 宗介：《悬崖上的金鱼公主》里的主人公小男孩。

7. **Hans Christian Andersen** 汉斯 · 克里斯蒂安 · 安徒生(**1805—1875**)：丹麦作家，诗人，因为他的童话故事而世界闻名。他最著名的童话故事有《拇指姑娘》、《卖火柴的小女孩》、《丑小鸭》等。他的作品已经被译为多种语言在全球出版发行，他的童话故事还被改编为大量影视动画作品。

8. ***Little Mermaid*** 安徒生的经典童话《海的女儿》(即《小美人鱼》)。

9. **protagonist** 主角，主要人物：参见 Chapter4-11。

10. draft 草稿，草图

11. Scene 场景：包含全部故事要素的视觉范围，通常包括开端、发展和结局。

12. dubbing 配音

13. filmmaker 电影工作者：制作电影的人，通常指导演。

14. animated feature film 动画长片电影

15. Studio Ghibli 吉卜力动画工作室：1985 年由宫崎骏和高畑勲共同创办。其工作室不仅出品动画电影，还接纳一些动画广告、音乐电视等题材。

16. Miramax Film Corp. 米拉麦克斯电影公司：哈维 · 韦恩斯坦(Harvey Weinstein)和鲍勃 · 韦恩斯坦(Bob Weinstein)两兄弟于 1979 年在美国水牛城(Buffalo)创立，并以其父母名字的组合(Max and Miriam)为公司命名。为美国最重要独立片商之一，曾经是世界十大电影公司之一，1993 年被华特 · 迪士尼公司并购，负责发行艺术性较高或较冷门的小众电影，近年来开始朝大众电影发展。2005 年 10 月，Bob Weinstein 与 Harvey Weinstein 兄弟离开了 Miramax，自立了新公司。米拉麦克斯电影公司的官方网址：www.miramax.com。

17. *Princess Mononoke* 《幽灵公主》：由吉卜力工作室 1997 推出的动画长篇电影，由德间书店制作，宫崎骏担任脚本和导演，铃木敏夫担任制片人，由音乐大师久石让作曲。

18. *Titanic* 《泰坦尼克号》：1997 年由 20 世纪福克斯公司(20th Century Fox)推出的经典电影。

19. Japanese Academy Awards 日本电影学院奖：1978 年成立，是日本各大电影奖中唯一通过电视直播颁奖典礼的奖项。与“日本电影蓝丝带奖”(Blue Ribbon Award)、“每日电影奖”(Mainichi Film Concours)、“电影旬报奖”(Kinema Junpo)并称为日本电影界 4 大电影奖。官方网址：www.japan-academy-prize.jp。

20. *Spirited Away* 《千与千寻》：吉卜力工作室 2001 年的动画作品，由宫崎骏担任编剧和导演，铃木敏夫担任制片人，由久石让配乐。本片赢得第 75 届奥斯卡金像奖最佳动画长片，第 21 届香港电影金像奖最佳亚洲电影奖，2002 年获得第 52 届柏林电影节金熊奖，这是金熊奖第一次把奖项授予一部动画电影。

21. Academy Award 学院奖：是奥斯卡奖(Oscars)的官方正式称谓，奖项致力于表彰在电影领域做出杰出贡献的优秀人才，由成立于 1927 年的美国电影艺术与科学学会(Academy of Motion Picture Arts and Sciences)颁发。参见 Chapter16-1。

22. box office 票房

23. ***Castle of Cagliostro*** 《鲁邦三世之卡里奥斯特罗城堡》： 1979 年 12 月，的动画电影上映，宫崎骏首部执导的动画电影作品。从此“鲁邦系列”成为日本动画的保留节目。官方网址：www.lupin-3rd.net。

24. ***Castle in the Sky*** 《天空之城》：吉卜力工作室于 1986 年推出的一部动画电影，宫崎骏导演，高畑勲担任制片。

25. ***Time*** 时代杂志：是美国的一本新闻周刊，创办于 1923 年，每期开辟有“封面人物”专栏，每年年底选出年度时代风云人物，是对该年最有影响力的人、事或物的报道。

Comprehensive Questions

1. How do you understand the connection between Ponyo and Andersen's The Little Mermaid?
2. In what way is the sea one of the main protagonists?
3. How do you understand the theme of Ponyo?
4. Narrate one of Hayao Miyazaki's works and conclude his achievements.

Further Reading

◎ ***The Art of Ponyo***

Author：Hayao Miyazaki

Publisher：VIZ Media LLC (2009)

◎ ***Starting Point: 1979~1996***

Author：Hayao Miyazaki

Publisher：VIZ Media LLC (2009)

◎ ***Hayao Miyazaki A Life in Anime***

Publisher：Cocoro Books (2008)

Web Links

www.ghibliworld.com

8 CHAPTER

Text

Henry Selick[1] Talks about *Coraline*: The Electricity of Life

After visiting the magnificent ***Coraline***[2] set up at **Laika**[3] in Portland last year and watching the completed movie that opens recently through **Focus Features**[4] - the first **stop-motion**[5] feature made in 3D, I finally had the chance to sit down with director Henry Selick last week to discuss his latest stop-motion journey.

Interview

Bill Desowitz: Let's begin with the wonderful advancements took advantage of on *Coraline*: the improved puppetry, with movable parts and silicone and better hair and fabric; the beautiful sets; the ability to shoot digitally and in 3-D, all contributing to a more tactile and immersive experience.

Henry Selick: That was a big part of shooting 3-D. When you're doing stop-motion and weighing it against the other formats, you're trying to determine its strengths and weaknesses. For me, the strengths are that it's all real stuff: it's all real props and miniaturized but the stuff really exists and 3-D captures that. I've often said we don't have the best movie in the business but we have the best tour.People would come visit us and would see these huge miniature sets with forests and trees all rigged with wires like they will move in the wind and the beautiful lighting. This feels like we finally captured that experience of what you get when you finally visit the film in production.

BD: Talk about the 3-D journey, which is significant in *Coraline*.

HS: I have a long history with 3-D -- I shot a 3-D rock video 20 years ago for the View-Master Corp. with **Lenny Lipton**[6]. Lenny is the godfather of the modern digital 3-D cinema.

BD: It's funny you have mentioned View-Master because that's just how I think of this whole new "immersive" approach to 3-D.

HS: That's what it goes back to: So I met Lenny and he's a genius and I would check in with him every few years and ask how it's developing. And going back to shooting ***Nightmare Before Christmas***[7] and ***James and the Giant Peach***[8], there were always a couple of 3-D hobbyists from our crew that would shoot stills in 3-D. And we just had this longing to shoot the stop-motion in 3-D. And then there was Lenny, who was developing how that might be and this long gestation period for *Coraline*, and in that time, getting to a stop-motion film and 3-D was happening, all these things started coming together. Ultimately, for a couple of years, I was looking to do The ***Wizard of Oz***[9] going from black-and-white to color. And so I thought that in a more subtle way, 3-D would really enhance the story, with Coraline discovering what appears to be a better world. And we actually designed the film for 3-D, changing the shapes of sets and so forth.

BD: Fortunately, I'm happy to report that most of your colleagues share your view. **Jeffrey Katzenberg**[10] says it's more about extending the proscenium rather than breaking it.

HS: I'm glad people are coming to the same conclusion.

BD: Let's talk about the experience of making *Coraline* at Laika with this particular crew.

HS: It's always a challenge to find enough people to do a stop-motion feature. It's not and will never be the dominant form of animation. But about one-third of our crew were veterans, going back to *Nightmare Before Christmas* and earlier. People I've worked with in some cases 20 years were: Bo Henry, Anthony Scott, Eric Leighton. So there was a solid of people that already knew how to communicate with one another. Then another one third were local artists and animators from Portland, Oregon. There's a long tradition of stop-motion with **Will Vinton**'s[11] company that specializes in **claymation**[12]. **Travis Knight**[13], one of our lead animators, is one of the best animators in the world, in the top five or 10 that I've ever worked with, so he set the bar very high for the local talent. And then one third was international: a lot of Brits, Canadians, Belgians, Germans, New Zealanders.

BD: You previously mentioned that you intentionally instructed everyone to be wary of trying to reach perfection.

HS: Well, in the past, when **Ray Harryhausen**[14] was doing his magnificent stop-motion monsters, creatures and effects for films, the attempt was to make it as realistic as possible. People were supposed to believe they were real and they did. But the world changed with ***Jurassic Park***[15], and then it changed again with ***Toy Story***[16]. And I've done a lot of soul searching over the years. What are the strengths of stop-motion? What should we try to hold on to? There are a lot of strengths: it's touched by the hand of the artist -- you can feel that. You can sense that life force, but it's imperfect. It can't be done perfectly -- that's what CG can do. And I'm trying to get people to embrace that: if it pops, if cloth shifts a little, if the hair is buzzing. It's like this electricity of life.

RAY HARRYHAUSEN

BD: And what other soul-searching have you done about stop-motion?

HS: Again, the question of playing to its strengths and what it can't do well. I felt that it's important to try and keep pushing it in terms of subject matter. A lot of people are concerned that is too scary. I actually think back to the first Disney films that deal with this very effectively: *Snow White*, ***Pinocchio***[17], ***Bambi***[18], ***Fantasia***[19]. It's ***Alice in Wonderland***[20] that meets **Grimms' fairy tale**[21]. In one respect, I'm going back to classic storytelling, which is at the heart of **Neil Gaiman**'s[22] book, but this time, the other animators aren't touching this territory, so, for me, it's breaking new ground. So part of my soul searching is taking stop-motion to new places: don't play following the leader. Look, I understand there's a lot of variety, especially at Pixar, in the stories that are being told, but the tone and feel of those films are very different from what I want to explore.

BD: What kinds of stories are you looking to tell?

HS: Not necessarily for me, but I just think animation can do so much and the film I most want to see that I haven't seen is ***Waltz with Bashir***[23].

BD: I finally caught up with it.

HS: What did you think?

BD: It's wonderful.

HS: See! I read about it and I've seen the images.

BD: And it really stays with you. It's such a provocative subject and has such a distinctive style.

HS: So I knew that done right, animation can take on a subject in that way. There are graphic novels being turned into live action and many of them should be animated. One thing: Travis Knight will be running a company up there. He has nothing against doing a **PG-13**[24] animated film. Why wouldn't we? If we find the story or create one and that's where it goes, great! Probably the majority of successful live action is PG-13. I don't understand why people don't take more risks, but at this point in history, taking chances on something new is actually the best bet. You'll never catch up with Pixar and **DreamWorks**[25] or Blue Sky. They're so good. But they're successful enough to take risks. Look at ***WALL-E***[26]. It breaks new ground, absolutely. And it's a very difficult thing to do a family-friendly film that breaks new ground. It's brilliant work they're doing, but I want to actually be a little bolder and we have to keep the costs down.

Words and Phrases

magnificent [mæg'nifisənt]
adj. 杰出的；壮丽的；华丽的

advancement [əd'vɑ:nsmənt]
n. 进步，进展

puppetry ['pʌpitri]
n. 木偶；木偶戏

silicone ['silikəun]
n. 硅树脂；硅酮

fabric ['fæbrik]
n. 织物；布

tactile ['tæktail, -til]
adj. 触觉的，有触觉的；能触知的

immersive [i'mə:siv]
adj. 身临其境

strength [streŋθ]
n. 优势；长处

weakness ['wi:knis]
n. 弱点

props [prɔps]
n. 小道具

miniaturize ['miniətʃəraiz]
v. 使小型化；使微型化

miniature ['miniətʃə]
n. 缩图；微型画；微型图画绘画术

rig [rig]
vt. 操纵；装配

wire ['waiə]
n. 电线；金属丝

significant [sig'nifikənt]
adj. 重大的；有效的；有意义的

hobbyist ['hɔbiist]
n. 业余爱好者；沉溺于某嗜好之人

crew [kru:]
n. 队，组；全体人员

longing ['lɔŋiŋ]
n. 渴望；憧憬

gestation period
孕期；酝酿期

ultimately ['ʌltimətli]
adv. 最后；基本上

look to
v. 注意

subtle ['sʌtl]
adj. 微妙的；精细的；敏感的

and so forth
等等，诸如此类

proscenium [prəu'si:njəm]
n. 舞台；舞台前部；舞台前部装置

dominant ['dɔminənt]
adj. 占优势的；支配的，统治的

veteran ['vetərən]
n. 老手；富有经验的人

in some cases
在某些情况下；有时候

Oregon ['ɔrigən]
n. 美国俄勒冈州

Brits [brits]
n. 英国人

Belgian ['beldʒən]
n. 比利时人

intentionally [in'tenʃənli]
adv. 故意地，有意地

be wary of
提防，当心

hold on to
坚持；紧握；克制

embrace [im'breis]
v. 拥抱；信奉，皈依

soul-searching
n. 深刻反省，自省，自我剖析

in terms of
依据；按照

scary ['skɛəri]
adj. 令人恐惧的，骇人的

territory ['teritəri]
n. 领域；范围

caught up with
被…迷住，入迷

provocative [prəu'vɔkətiv]
adj. 刺激的，挑拨的

distinctive [dis'tiŋktiv]
adj. 有特色的，与众不同的

risk [risk]
n. 风险

take chances
冒险

best bet
最好的办法、途径

bold [bəuld]
adj. 大胆的，英勇的

Notes

1. **Henry Selick** 亨利·塞利克 ：美国动画导演，1952年生于美国新泽西，毕业于加州艺术学院，后进入迪士尼。导演的长篇动画电影作品有《飞天巨桃历险记》(*James and the Giant Peach*)、《圣诞夜惊魂》(*Nightmare Before Christmas*)、《鬼妈妈》(*Coraline*)等作品。

2. ***Coraline*** 《鬼妈妈》：又译为《卡洛琳》，亨利 · 塞利克(Henry Selick)2006年导演的动画电影，根据尼尔·盖曼(Neil Caiman)同名小说改编。获得第37届动画安妮奖(Annie Awards)提名。

3. **Laika** 莱卡动画工作室：2005年建于美国俄勒冈州的波特兰(Portland)，致力于动画长片电影和影视广告领域的探索，其作品多次获得包括奥斯卡奖、艾美奖在内的多项大奖。《鬼妈妈》(*Coraline*)是工作室的第一部长篇动画电影作品。官方网址：www.laika.com。

4. **Focus Features** 焦点电影公司：2004 年 5 月成立，隶属于环球电影公司，作品有 2009 年的《机器人 9 号》(*Nine*)等作品。

5. **stop-motion** 定格动画：也称停格动画或逐格动画，是一种以手工制作的人物模型为对象，应用摄影技术来制作的一种动画形式。定格动画有别于传统动画和电脑动画，具有非常高的艺术表现性和真实的材质纹理。

6. **Lenny Lipton** 连尼·利普顿：著名的作家、电影制片人以及立体视觉系统发明家。

7. ***Nightmare Before Christmas*** 《圣诞夜惊魂》：亨利 · 塞利克(Henry Selick)执导的长篇定格动画电影。影片古怪风趣，略带恐怖色彩，采用百老汇歌剧风格配合阴沉的画面，呈现出蒂姆·伯顿式的黑色喜剧风格。

8. ***James and the Giant Peach*** 《飞天巨桃历险记》：1996 年由提姆·波顿改编为同名动画电影，亨利 · 塞利克 (Henry Selick)执导。

9. ***Wizard of Oz*** 《绿野仙踪》：根据同名童话改编的经典儿童音乐电影，由维克多·弗莱明(Victor Fleming)执导，1939 年在美国上映。

10. **Jeffrey Katzenberg** 杰弗瑞 · 卡森伯格：1950 年生于纽约市，美国著名电影制片人兼梦工厂动画制作公司行政总裁，“DreamWorks SKG”中的“K”就代表了他。

11. **Will Vinton** 威尔 · 文顿：1948 年出生于美国俄勒冈州，20 世纪 70 年代早期进入加州大学柏克莱分校学习，对西班牙建筑大师安东尼奥 · 高迪(Antonio Gaudi)的作品十分迷恋，欣赏其艺术作品呈现的流动设计感，受此影响开始黏土动画实验创作。1974 年，威尔 · 文顿完成九分钟动画短片《周一公休》(*Closed Mondays*)，获得 1975 年奥斯卡最佳动画短片奖。1977 至 1979 年间，威尔 · 文顿根据俄罗斯文学巨匠托尔斯泰(Leo Tolstoy)的文学作品改编创作了《补鞋匠马丁》(*Martin the Cobbler*)；根据美国文学家华盛顿 · 欧文(Washington Irving)的作品改编创作了《李伯大梦》(*Rip Van Winkle*)；根据法国文学家安东尼 · 德 · 圣 · 埃克苏佩里(Antoine De Saint-Exupery)的名著改编创作《小王子》(*The Little Prince*)，这三部动画短片后来集结成三部曲。1985 年，威尔·文顿完成了世界动画史上第一部全黏土动画长片《马克 · 吐温历险记》(*The Adventures of Mark Twain*)。2002 年，威尔·文顿在专注于原有黏土动画制作导演之外，开始计算机动画的创作。威尔·文顿的黏土动画使用了专业的彩色橡胶黏土(plasticine clay)技术，为世界动画发展做出了杰出贡献。官方网址：www.willvinton.net。

12. **claymation** 黏土动画：定格动画的一种，它由逐帧拍摄制作而成，它是用黏土或橡皮泥等可塑材质来制作人物，一般运用金属骨架来控制角色的造型和姿态。在前期制作过程中，依靠大量手工制作，使黏土动画具有淳朴、自然的艺术特色。比较著名的作品包括阿德曼公司(Aardman Animations)的“酷狗宝贝系列”(*Wallace and Gromit*)、《小鸡快跑》(*Chicken Run*)、《玛丽和马克思》(*Mary and Max*)等。

13. **Travis Knight** 特拉维斯 · 奈特：动画电影《鬼妈妈》(*Coraline*)的视觉特效师，被亨利 · 塞利克(Henry Selick)极力推崇的人物。

14. **Ray Harryhausen** 雷 · 哈里豪森：定格动画大师、电影视觉特效大师。1920 年 5 月 29 日生于美国洛杉矶，20 世纪 40 年代初进入电影界，首先跟随乔治 · 帕尔(George Pal)摄制木偶短片集。第二次世界大战后，在电影特技专家威利斯 · 奥布赖恩(Wills O'brien)手下协助制作了《巨猩乔扬》(*Mighty Joe Young*)，该片获得 1949 年奥斯卡金像奖最佳特效。1952 年，担任华纳兄弟影片公司科学幻想片《原子怪兽》(*The Beast From 20,000 Fathoms*)的特效工作。2001，为表彰哈里豪森为美国电影特效领域作出的巨大贡献，获得了在温哥华举行的"视觉效果动画节"的视觉特效终身成就大奖。官方网址：www.rayharryhausen.com。

15. ***Jurassic Park***《侏罗纪公园》：由史蒂文 · 斯皮尔伯格(Steven Spielberg)于 1993 年执导的电影特效领域的经典名作，此片至 2007 年为止名列全球票房榜前十名之列，之后发展成系列电影。

16. ***Toy Story***《玩具总动员》：约翰 · 拉塞特(John Lasseter)导演作品，由华特 · 迪士尼影片公司(Walt Disney Pictures)和皮克斯动画工作室(Pixar Animation Studios)合作推出。此片是首部完全使用电脑动画技术绘制的动画长片，于 1995 年 11 月在北美公映。影片另外发行有电影音乐原声带、游戏和玩具等周边产品。

17. ***Pinocchio*** 《木偶奇遇记》：是意大利童话作家科洛迪(Carlo Collodi)的代表作，发表于 1880 年。该作品于 1940 年被迪士尼公司改编为动画电影，后分别于 1983 年和 2002 年翻拍真人版。

18. ***Bambi*** 《小鹿斑比》：是迪士尼最成功的卡通片之一，于 1942 年上映。

19. ***Fantasia***《幻想曲》：1940 年上映，影片将古典音乐与动画完美结合，是世界第一部立体音响的电影，在影史上占有非常重要的地位。此片获第 14 届奥斯卡特别成就奖(音乐和录音技术两项金像奖)。

20. ***Alice in Wonderland*** 《爱丽丝梦游仙境》：迪士尼出品的动画电影，于 1951 年上映。故事取材自英国作家路易斯 · 卡罗尔(Lewis Carroll)1865 年出版的儿童文学作品，对后世文学、电影创作产生了极大影响。2010 年，蒂姆 · 波顿(Tim Burton)版的《爱丽丝梦游仙境》在全球上映。

21. **Grimms' fairy tale** 格林童话

22. **Neil Gaiman** 尼尔 · 盖曼：动画电影《鬼妈妈》(*Coraline*)的原创文学作者。1960 年出生于英格兰的犹太裔作家，写作领域跨越科幻长短篇小说、图像小说、漫画及剧本编写。

23. ***Waltz with Bashir*** 《和巴什尔跳华尔兹》：由以色列导演阿里 · 福尔曼(Ari Folman)执导的动画电影，2008 年上映。影片中导演试图给观众还原他对 1982 年贝鲁特难民营大屠杀(Beirut camps)的记忆。本片获得 2008 年恺撒奖(Caesar award)最佳外语片奖，金球奖(Golden Globe Awards)最佳外语片奖，奥斯卡(Oscar)最佳外语片提名，英国电影电视艺术学会(BAFTA)最佳非英语影片和最佳动画片奖。

24. PG-13 美国的电影分级，指 13 岁以下儿童要有父母陪同观看的影片。

25. DreamWorks SKG 梦工厂：始建于 1994 年 10 月，是美国电影洗印、制作和发行公司，同时也是一家游戏和电视节目制作公司。三位创始人分别是史蒂文 · 斯皮尔伯格(Steven Allan Spielberg)、 杰弗瑞 · 卡森伯格(Jeffrey Katzenberg)和大卫 · 格芬(David Geffen)，SKG 为三个人的名字缩写。制作的动画作品包括《马达加斯加》(*Madagascar*)、《功夫熊猫》(*Kung Fu Panda*)、《怪物史莱克》(*Shrek*)系列等脍炙人口的作品。

26. ***WALL · E*** 《机器人总动员》：是皮克斯动画工作室被迪士尼收购后出品的又一部动画电影，获第 81 届奥斯卡最佳动画长片奖。

Comprehensive Questions

1. What changes did 3-D bring to Coraline?
2. What was Selick's biggest concern when he was doing soul-searching?
3. In some sense Selick was taking risks. What do you think made him hold on?
4. "The Electricity of Life"——how do you understand the title of the text?

Further Reading

◎*Coraline: A Visual Companion*

Author：Stephen Jones

Publisher：It Books; Mti edition (2009)

◎ ***Tim Burton's Nightmare Before Christmas***

Author：Frank Thompson

Publisher：Disney Enterprises, Inc (2002)

Web Links

www.coraline.com

9 CHAPTER

Text

Aardman Animation Studio

Aardman Animations, Ltd.[1], also known as Aardman Studios, is an Academy Award-winning British animation studio based in Bristol, United Kingdom. The studio is famous for its stop-motion, **clay animation**[2] productions, particularly those featuring plasticine duo ***Wallace & Gromit***[3].

Peter Lord and David Sproxton[4] began their animating partnership at school. In 1972 they registered the name Aardman Animations. After graduating, they moved to Bristol in 1976 where they created **Morph**[5] for the children's programme. Peter and David met **Nick Park**[6] at the **National Film and Television School**[7] when he was working on his student film ***A Grand Day Out***[8]. He joined Aardman full time in 1985. In 1986, **Peter Gabriel**[9] suggested that they collaborate with director Stephen Johnson and the **Brothers Quay**[10] to create a new rock video. ***Sledgehammer***[11] went on to collect many awards that year. That original combination of rhythm, energy, style and visual flair was also harnessed to provide the visual accompaniment to the late **Nina Simone**[12]'s *My Baby Just Cares For Me* and **Robert Parker**[13]'s *Barefootin*.

In 1989 the studio was again commissioned by **Channel Four Television**[14] to create a series of five 5-minute films, ***Lip Synch***[15]. This ground-breaking series further explored the world of animation based on true characters and real voices and included Peter Lord's *War Story* and *Going Equipped*, **Barry Purves**[16]' *Next*, **Richard Goleszowski**[17]'s *Ident* and Nick Park's *Creature Comforts*.

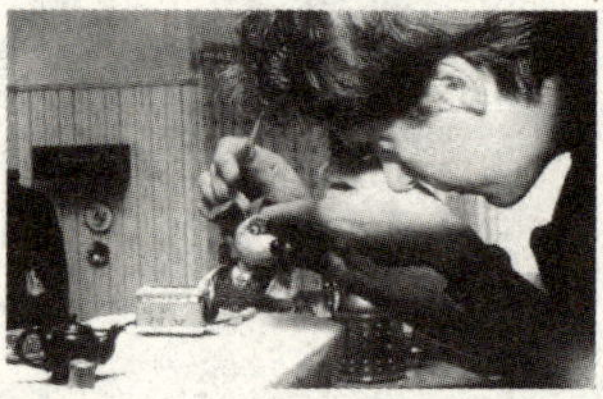

In 1993 Aardman passed another milestone with the completion of Nick Park's Oscar winning ***The Wrong Trousers***[18], Aardman's first 30 minute film. Acclaimed world-wide winner of over thirty awards, *The Wrong Trousers* has become one of the most successful animated films ever made. In 1995 Aardman produced Nick Park's third Oscar winning film ***A Close Shave***[19]. An immediate success, it confirmed the studio's reputation as well as establishing *Wallace and Gromit* as household names. In 1996 the studio produced Peter Lord's Oscar nominated 11' short film, ***Wat's Pig***[20].

In 1998, Aardman won a **BAFTA**[21] for ***Stage Fright***[22], an 11minute short film commissioned by Channel Four Television. **Steve Box**[23], Nick Park's **key animator**[24] on both *The Wrong Trousers* and *A Close Shave*, directed *Stage Fright*.

The studio's first animated television series for youth and adults, ***Rex The Runt***[25], created and directed by Aardman associate Richard Goleszowski, was first shown on BBC2 in 1998 and garnered many top international awards. A second series was commissioned and shown on BBC2 in 2001. ***Angry Kid***[26], directed by Darren Walsh, was Aardman's first series released exclusively on the internet, via **Atomfilms**[27].com.

Chicken Run[28] was Aardman's first full-length theatrical feature film to be funded by DreamWorks. Directed by both Peter Lord and Nick Park it was released in June 2000 in the US and UK to excellent reviews and outstanding **box office**[29] receipts. *Chicken Run* grossed over $220M at the worldwide box office. In autumn 2002

Aardman released ***Cracking Contraptions***[30], a series of 10 x 1 minute Wallace and Gromit films. The films debuted on the Internet and were viewed by hundreds of thousands of people world-wide. All 10 films were then shown on BBC1 over the 2002 autumn and Christmas schedule. The films were also released online in the US via AtomFilms who went on to offer a subscription package for all ten.

To mass critical acclaim and outstanding box office results, Wallace and Gromit's first feature film ***The Curse of the Were-Rabbit***[31] was released by DreamWorks in October 2005. The film topped the box office charts both in US and UK and garnered many prestigious international awards including the Academy Award for Best Animated Feature Film and a BAFTA for Best British Film.

Flushed Away[32], the studio's first CG film was released worldwide by DreamWorks in November 2006. It was nominated for a BAFTA in 2007. Aardman's television series, ***Shaun the Sheep***[33] debuted on BBC1 and **CBBC**[34] in March 2007. Inspired by Nick Park's 1995 Academy Award winning short film *A Close Shave*, the series has been sold worldwide. *Wallace and Gromit*'s latest adventure ***A Matter of Loaf and Death***[35] was broadcast on BBC One on Christmas day 2008 and enthralled a record audience of 16.15M. It went on to win the BAFTA for Best Animated Short Film. *Wallace and Gromit* currently feature in a major exhibition at the Science Museum in London. ***Timmy Time***[36], Aardman's first pre-school TV production debuted on **CBeebies**[37] in April 2009.

Two feature films are currently in production via Aardman's deal with SONY Pictures. ***Arthur Christmas***[38] - an action-adventure comedy set on Christmas Eve is scheduled for release in 2011 and ***Pirates! - In an Adventure With Scientists***[39] will be released in 2012. A number of other feature films are in development. From Peter and David's tabletop beginnings, Aardman has grown into a major, world class studio. Their work continues to be innovative, entertaining, brilliant and full of charm, reflecting the talent, energy and personal commitment of all the people who comprise the Aardman team.

Words and Phrases

Bristol ['bristəl]
布里斯托尔，英国西南部重要海港城市，历史悠久、环境宜人

plasticine ['plæstəsi:n]
n. 橡皮泥；塑像用黏土

register ['redʒistə]
v. 登记；注册

rhythm ['riðəm, 'riθəm]
n. 节奏；韵律

harness ['hɑ:nis]
v. 用来；驾驭；制约

commission [kə'miʃən]
v. 委任；委托制作

ground-breaking
adj. 独创的；开拓性的

milestone ['mailstəun]
n. 里程碑，划时代的事件

confirm [kən'fə:m]
vt. 确认；使巩固

reputation [,repju'teiʃən]
n. 名声，名誉；声望

garner ['gɑ:nə]
vt. 获得

debut ['deibju:]
vi. 初次登台；首播

mass [mæs]
v. 集中；聚集

prestigious [pre'stidʒəs]
adj. 有名望的；享有声望的

enthrall [in'θrɔ:l]
vt. 迷住，吸引住

comedy ['kɔmidi]
n. 喜剧；喜剧性；有趣的事情

innovative ['inəuveitiv]
adj. 革新的，创新的

entertaining [,entə'teiniŋ]
adj. 令人愉快的

brilliant ['briljənt]
adj. 灿烂的；辉煌的

Notes

1. **Aardman Animations, Ltd.** 阿德曼动画工作室：著名的定格动画制作工作室，由大卫 · 史波克斯顿(David Sproxton)和搭档彼得 · 罗德(Peter Lord)于 1972 年以 Aardman Animations 的名字注册。公司旗下最负盛名的动画作品是尼克 · 帕克(Nick Park)执导的“超级无敌掌门狗系列”，曾赢得多项国际动画大奖，其作品以特殊的英国风格、轻松幽默的人物刻画和精致的拍摄品质著称于世。官方网址：www.aardman.com。

2. **clay animation** 黏土动画：参见 Chapter7-13。

3. ***Wallace & Gromit*** 阿德曼工作室著名导演尼克 · 帕克(Nick Park)创作的“超级无敌掌门狗系列”中的经典形象。作品描写了一只叫做阿高(Gromit)的小狗和它的主人华莱士(Wallace)之间的层出不穷的奇特冒险经历。

4. **Peter Lord，David Sproxton** 彼得 · 罗德和大卫 · 史波克斯顿 1972 年共同创立了著名的阿德曼动画工作室，联合创作了旗下众多经典动画作品，如《小鸡快跑》(*Chicken Run*)等，2009 年获得 BAFTA 特别大奖。

5. **Morph** 1976 年阿德曼动画工作室搬到布里斯托尔(Bristol)的同时为 BBC 儿童节目创作了他们第一个成功的动画人物——摩夫(Morph)，一个造型简单、永远面带微笑的胶泥动画人物。该作品为阿德曼日后黏土动画的成功创作奠定了基础。

6. **Nick Park** 尼克·帕克：是阿德曼动画工作室旗下著名的动画导演。1958 生于英国普雷斯顿(Preston)，1980 年毕业于英国谢菲尔德工艺学校的传媒艺术专业(Communication Arts at Sheffield Polytechnic)，1980 年到 1983 年在英国国家电影电视学校(National Film & Television School)学习动画电影制作。1985 年加入阿德曼工作室，并完成了《月球野餐记》(*A Grand Day Out*)的创作，此片为尼克 · 帕克赢得了 1990 年英国学院奖(BAFTA Awards)最佳动画片，1991 年奥斯卡最佳动画短片奖提名等多项大奖。

7. **National Film and Television School(NFTS)** 英国国家电影电视学校，位于英国贝康斯斐(Beaconsfield)，提供独具特色的影视教育课程，是一所享有国际声誉的影视学校。校友遍布全球电视、电影和传媒行业。官方网址：www.nftsfilm-tv.ac.uk。

8. ***A Grand Day Out***《月球野餐记》：又译作《奇异的假期》，阿德曼工作室早期著名动画短片，尼克 · 帕克(Nick Park)导演的“超级无敌掌门狗系列”的第一集。

9. **Peter Gabriel** 彼得 · 盖布瑞尔：1950 年生于伦敦，是 1970 年代“创世纪”(Genesis)摇滚乐团的团长，从早期的非主流前卫曲风，到后来成为一位流行音乐巨星。

10. **Brothers Quay** 奎氏兄弟：孪生兄弟史蒂芬 · 奎(Stephen Quay)和蒂莫西 · 奎(Timothy Quay)，1947 年生于美国费城(Philadelphia)，毕业于宾夕法尼亚艺术大学，对欧洲(尤其是东欧)文化有着浓厚兴趣，1969—1972 年在伦敦王室艺术学院(Royal College of Arts)学习并开始制作短片。1978 年成立 Koninck 工作室，创作定格动画电影。

11. ***Sledgehammer***《大锤》：阿德曼公司的早期作品，是为英国摇滚歌手彼得 ·盖布瑞尔(Peter Gabriel)拍摄的音乐录像带，影片画面丰富具有节奏感，是一部充满想象力的作品。

12. **Nina Simone** 妮娜 · 西蒙**(1933—2003)**：美国女歌手、作曲家与钢琴表演家，演唱方式富有情感，代表作有《我的宝贝只在乎我》(*My Baby Just Cares For Me*)。

13. **Robert Parker** 罗伯特 · 帕克：美国蓝调歌手与音乐家，1930 年出生于美国新奥尔良(NewOrleans)，代表作有 1966 年的《赤足而行》(*Barefootin*)。

14. **Channel Four Television** 英国电视台第四频道：紧跟新媒体变革潮流，结合互联网、手机和电视等，自创许多互联网音视频节目，在新媒体领域独树一帜，在英国传媒业产生了非常大的影响。官方网址：www.Channel4.com。

15. ***Lip Synch*** 《同期录音》：阿德曼公司于 1989 年至 1990 年制作的五集动画系列片，其中尼克 · 帕克导演的《动物物语》(*Creature Comforts*，又译作《物质享受》)为公司夺得了第一个奥斯卡最佳动画短片奖；彼得 · 罗德(Peter Lord)的《战争故事》(*War Story*)获得英国学院奖(BAFTA Award)。

16. **Barry Purves** 巴瑞 · 普维斯：阿德曼工作室导演，代表作有 1989 年的《下一个》(*Next*)。1992 年离开阿德曼动画公司，利用日本传统戏剧形式 Kabuki 制作了木偶动画片《剧本》(*Screen Play*)，获得奥斯卡最佳动画短片奖提名。

17. **Richard Goleszowski** 理查德 · 哥勒斯索斯基：阿德曼工作室导演，2007 年执导了《小羊肖恩》(*Shaun the Sheep*)。

18. ***The Wrong Trousers***《引鹅入室》：又译为《错误的裤子》，是尼克 · 帕克导演的"超级无敌掌门狗系列"第二集，获得 1994 年奥斯卡最佳动画短片奖。

19. ***A Close Shave*** 《剃刀边缘》：阿德曼 1995 年推出的动画短片作品，获得 1996 年奥斯卡最佳动画短片奖。

20. ***Wat's Pig*** 《双胞胎传奇》：阿德曼工作室 1996 年拍摄的经典动画作品，彼得 · 罗德(Peter Lord)编剧和导演。

21. **BAFTA (British Academy of Film and Television Arts)**英国电影电视艺术学会：创建于 1947 年，总部设在伦敦，机构颁发电影领域的重要奖项——英国电影和电视艺术学会奖，通常被称为英国学院奖，官方网址：www.bafta.org。 注意要把它和英国其他的电影教育机构区分开，英国电影学院的英文名称是 British Film Institute(BFI)，官方网址：www.bfi.org.uk；英国国家电影电视学校的英文名称是 National Film and Television School(NFTS)，官方网址：www.nftsfilm-tv.ac.uk。

22. ***Stage Fright*** 《怯场》：阿德曼导演史蒂夫 · 博克斯(Steve Box)于 1997 年执导的 11 分钟动画短片作品。

23. **Steve Box** 史蒂夫 · 博克斯：阿德曼公司的著名动画导演，2005 年与尼克 · 帕克联合执导了《超级无敌掌门狗：人兔的诅咒》(*Wallace & Gromit in The Curse of the Were-Rabbit*)，该片获得 2006 年奥斯卡最佳动画长片奖。

24. **key animator** 关键帧画师：参见 Chapter2-28。

25. ***Rex The Runt*** 《小犬雷克斯》：阿德曼工作室首部面向全年龄段的长篇电视动画系列，由理查德•哥勒斯索斯基(Richard Goleszowski)执导。1998 年在 BBC2 首播，赢得多项国际奖项。

26. ***Angry Kid*** 阿德曼工作室 1999 年至 2000 年推出的动画作品，由戴伦 · 沃什(Darren Walsh)执导，是阿德曼第一部完全借由 Atom Film(www.atomfilms.com)网站发布的动画作品。

27. **Atomfilms** 原子影业公司：创建人 Mika Salmi，原子影业的主要工作就是帮助那些业余电影制作者，通过公司的网站把他们制作的短片推向一个比较广阔的受众群体。官方网址：www.atomfilms.com。

28. ***Chicken Run*** 《小鸡快跑》：阿德曼工作室第一部动画长片作品，由彼得 ·罗德(Peter Lord)和尼克 · 帕克(Nick Park)共同执导，2000 年由美国梦工厂(DreamWorks SKG)发行，创造了当年的票房佳绩。这是阿德曼工作室与梦工厂合作的首部在影院上映的标准长度动画长片。获得英国动画奖(British Animation Awards)最佳欧洲故事片奖(Best European Feature Film)等多项大奖。

29. **box office** 票房

30. ***Cracking Contraptions*** 《疯狂发明》：阿德曼工作室 2002 年推出的十集系列动画短片，原子影业(AtomFilms)的网站上首先提供本片的在线收看，2002 年秋天和圣诞节期间在 BBC1 台播出。

31. ***The Curse of the Were-Rabbit*** 《超级无敌掌门狗：人兔的诅咒》：由史蒂夫 · 博克斯(Steve Box)和尼克 · 帕克 (Nick Park)执导，梦工厂(DreamWorks SKG)发行。该片获得了 2006 年奥斯卡最佳动画片奖和英国学院奖(BAFTA)最佳英国电影等众多国际大奖。

32. ***Flushed Away*** 《鼠国流浪记》：阿德曼公司与梦工厂(DreamWorks SKG)合作发行的第三部动画长片，也是阿德曼工作室首部 CG 动画电影，由大卫 · 鲍沃斯(David Bowers)和山姆 · 菲尔(Sam Fell)执导，获得 2007 年英国学院奖(BAFTA)提名。

33. ***Shaun the Sheep*** 电视动画《小羊肖恩》：2007 年在 BBC1 和 CBBC 首播。肖恩(Shaun)这一角色首次在尼克 · 帕克 1995 年作品《剃刀边缘》(*A Close Shave*)中出现。

34. **CBBC** 英国广播公司儿童频道：于 2002 年 2 月开播，CBBC 原是英国广播公司旗下的数字频道 BBC 选择频道(BBC Choice)上的一个少儿节目板块，后来演变成一个单独的数字频道，提倡节目的原创与人文内涵。

35. ***A Matter of Loaf and Death*** 《超级无敌掌门狗：面包与死亡事件》：是“超级无敌掌门狗”系列第五部作品。获得 2009 年英国学院奖(BAFTA)最佳动画短片奖和 2010 年奥斯卡最佳动画短片奖提名。

36. ***Timmy Time*** 《蒂咪时间》：阿德曼工作室首部为学龄前儿童制作的电视动画片，2009年4月在 CBeebies 频道播出。

37. CBeebies 由英国 BBC 推出的儿童频道。官方网址：www.bbc.co.uk/cbeebies。

38. ***Arthur Christmas*** 《亚瑟·圣诞》：阿德曼公司 2011 年推出的 CG 动画作品，影片由莎拉·史密斯(Sarah Smith)和巴里·库克(Barry Cook)共同执导。

39. ***Pirates! - In An Adventure With Scientists*** 《海盗——与科学家的一次冒险》：阿德曼公司计划于 2012 年推出的动画作品，是与索尼(Sony Pictures)新合作关系中的首部企划作品，将由彼得·罗德(**Peter Lord**)执导。

Comprehensive Questions

1. Of all the Aardman Studio's products mentioned in the text, which one do you like best? Give your reasons.
2. If you were given the chance to work for Aardman Studio, in what ways would you prepare yourself?

Further Reading

◎ ***Creating 3-D Animation----The Aardman Book of Filmmaking***

Author：Peter Lord, Brian Sibley, Aardman Animations

Publisher：HARRY N. ABRAMS INC. (1998)

◎ ***The World of Wallace and Gromit***

Author：Andy Lane

Publisher：Boxtree Ltd (2004)

◎ ***The Art of Wallace and Gromit***

Publisher：Egmont Books Ltd (2009)

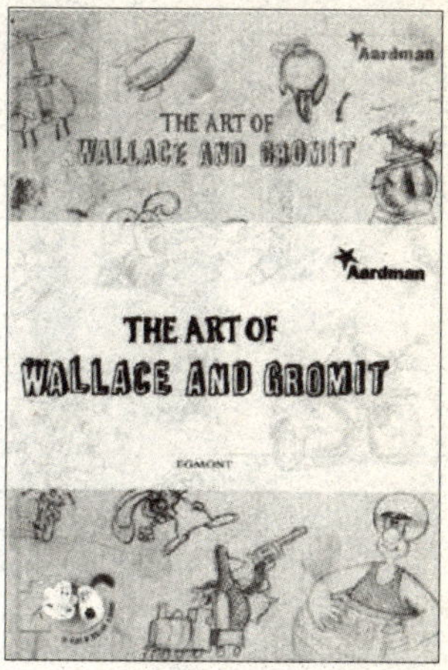

Web Links

www.aardman.com

www.wallaceandgromit.com

10 CHAPTER

Text

Te Wei and Chinese Animation

Te Wei[1] (August 22, 1915 - February 4, 2010) was a Chinese animator. He was known for his traditional style of art, and was considered one of the founders of Chinese animation. He worked in animation for several decades and won several awards for his work. He has the credit of being the only Chinese artist to be awarded the Lifetime Achievement Award by the **International Animated Film Association**[2].

In 1956, while directing The ***Conceited General***[3], Te Wei hung a slogan on the studio wall to urge animators to explore a Chinese characteristic animation creation way. The *Conceited General* was the first experiment in Chinese-style animation with its Peking opera-like movements. Te Wei said, "We had a clear idea to draw useful things from the traditional arts -- local opera, drama, Peking opera. From the models to the movements, we followed these operas. Most importantly, we invited opera teachers to the film studio to show us how to move."

As The *Conceited General* and other animated films with prominent Chinese styles became popular in art circles and society at large, the experimentation was accelerated, not only on content and techniques, but also on basic raw material. Te

Wei explained, "We made paper cut and puppet as these were plentiful materials from Chinese culture. We have a long tradition of paper cut and **shadow puppetry**[4], and we made paper cut animation very successfully." Wan Guchan, one of the brothers who started Chinese animation, and **Hu Jinqing**[5] worked for a year to make the first paper cut-out film, ***Piggy (Zhu Bajie) Eats the Watermelon***[6] (1958) award.

From 1960s his animation style was influenced by the painter **Qi Baishi**[7]. The film, ***Where Is Mama?***[8] (1960), won five awards, including those at **Annecy**[9], **Cannes**[10] and **Locarno**[11]. Te Wei wrote the script and directed a second water and ink film in 1963, ***Buffalo Boy and the Flute***[12]. And later served as the general director of ***Feelings from Mountain and Water***[13](1988) which won five prizes, including grand prizes on **Montreal**[14] and **Shanghai International Film Festivals**[15]. In 1995, ASIFA gave Te Wei a Lifetime Achievement Award . "The award means I can draw a dot to my career," he said, but adding, "I think I can do more to make animation unique." At 86, he said he is waiting for a good script to direct, implying it might be a water and ink production, because he thought this technique was unique and should be preserved.

In 1999, the government selected the 100 outstanding films of China; only 20 animation works were represented and Te Wei's four were among them. Also, as a leader of the animation industry, Te Wei had three accomplishments:

1. He founded a Chinese national style of animation;

2. He established a highly talented group: under his leadership, the **Shanghai Animation Film Studio**[16] developed from several to hundreds of staff, uniting seniors like the Wan brothers and cultivating the younger generation of animators;

3. He led both of China's golden eras of animation and most of the famous Chinese animation were completed when he was the leader.

Interview

Question: Of all the Chinese arts, why were **water and ink**[17], paper cut, folding paper, and puppet adapted to animation?

Te Wei: In the 1950s, we thought we should made Chinese art films. The first animation was puppet. They were not called cartoons, but **art films**[18]. The staff at the time seldom said we should learn from Disney, but most of them liked Disney skills in movement, styles, etc. The word animation includes all aspects such as paper cut, paper fold, puppet, etc. We didn't waste time on how to call it; we just did things to make a national identity type animation. We also learned from the high skills of foreign countries. A problem now is that seldom do animators make deep research on foreign animation.

Q: What are you most proud of in your life?

TW: Most of my life has been connected with animation, and in the past decades, I did one important thing. I explored national styles and ways for animation -- water and ink films. But hardly can I feel satisfied; I always felt that there were defects in my works. It's a common phenomenon for directors to have regrets when they finish a film. At that time, film companies gave us money to do water and ink animation, and we were very happy to have that strong government support. Another deed I'm proud of was I organized talented people.

Q: What else will you do if you have the chance?

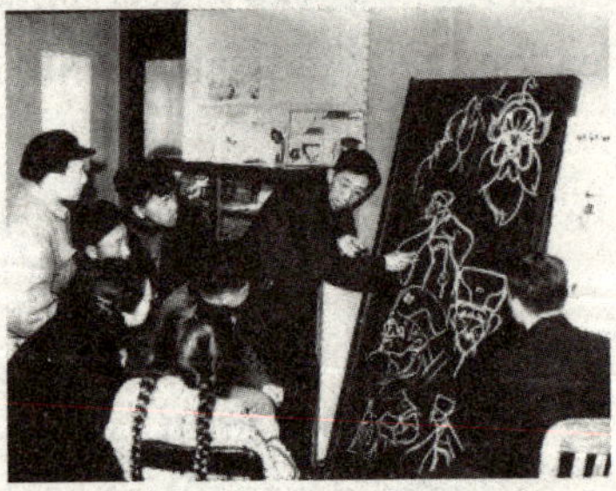

TW: I'm very strict with my own works. When I made films, I did not pay attention to audience reaction. That made me regretted. Next time, I would do better.

Q: What is the biggest artistic change in animation in the past 50 years?

TW: It is hard to say what the big artistic changes were. Artistic skills keep being promoted, and animation production keeps going smoothly; there are no ups and downs artistically.

Q: What are the characteristics that distinguish Chinese animation from that of other countries?

TW: Since 1956, I mentioned Chinese animation should find its own characteristics which I searched constantly until I retired in 1988 (after directing *Feelings*). This way is still going smoothly. It is still different from foreign animation. After 1980, Chinese animators attended international animation festivals, and China had its own; during the time, Chinese animators had a chance to open their eyes and found they lacked certain skills.

Through international animation festivals, foreign animators know more about Chinese animation; on the other hand, Chinese animators learn from the outside. Because of these observations of foreign works, Chinese animators are not satisfied with doing traditional animation. They know they have to learn other skills and when they learn good things from foreigners, some bad things come in.

Q: What has been learned from foreigners?

TW: When I was working, I paid more attention to creation. Now, retired, I feel some animators do more work for foreign companies; it's not their work, not Chinese animation. This is a bad impact. This situation has been around for years, not just recently. Chinese animators have tried to do something about the foreign works. Shanghai Animation Film Studio recently made ***Lotus Lantern***[19] which had market success. You can see Disney in it, but at least they tried. Few films are like that these days; it is not common to make efforts at high quality animation like *Lotus Lantern*. The artistic exploration and atmosphere are insufficient. Artistically and commercially, *Lotus Lantern* made contributions. We should not expect too much from these films, because it's difficult for animators to do exploration they need. Nowadays, the worldwide animation competition is stronger and stronger. Chinese animators should take bigger steps like *Lotus Lantern*. Disney has its ways and methods; Chinese animation must have its own characteristics to compete. But Disney and DreamWorks are too powerful and it is not easy to catch up with them.

Words and Phrases

decade ['dekeid]
n. 十年

slogan ['sləugən]
n. 标语

invite [in'vait, 'invait]
vt. 邀请

prominent ['prɔminənt]
adj. 杰出的；卓越的

art circles
艺术圈，艺术界

raw material
原料；原材料

paper cut
剪纸

plentiful ['plentiful]
adj. 丰富的；许多的

serve as
担任…，充当…

imply [im'plai]
vt. 意味；暗示

unique [ju:'ni:k]
adj. 独特的，稀罕的；唯一的

preserve [pri'zə:v]
v. 保护；防护；维护

accomplishment [ə'kʌmpliʃmənt]
n. 成就，造诣；本领

cultivate ['kʌltiveit]
vt. 培养；陶冶；耕作

defect ['di:fekt]
n. 缺点，缺陷；不足之处

phenomenon [fi'nɔminən]
n. 现象

regret [ri'gret]
n. 遗憾

talented ['tæləntid]
adj. 有才能的；多才的

be strict with
要求严格

go smoothly
进展顺利

observation [,ɔbzə:'veiʃən]
n. 观察；记录；学习

make effort
作出努力

compete [kəm'pi:t]
vi. 竞争；比赛

catch up with
赶上，追上

Notes

1. **Te Wei** 特伟 **(1915.8.22—2010.2.4)**：原名盛松，广东中山人，生于上海。水墨动画创始人之一，是新中国动画事业的主要奠基人。1949 年在长春电影制片厂负责组建美术片组，1950 年该组迁至上海，并于 1957 年建成上海美术电影制片厂。代表作有《好朋友》(1954)、《骄傲的将军》(1956)、《小蝌蚪找妈妈》(1960)、《牧笛》(1963)、《金猴降妖》(1984)、《山水情》(1988)等。作品获得国内外多项大奖，是中国唯一获得过“ASIFA 终身成就奖”的艺术家。

2. **International Animated Film Association (ASIFA)** 国际动画电影协会：1960 年创建于法国，目前轮值总部在克罗地亚，是全球性的国际动画艺术组织，在全球 30 多个国家设有分支机构。ASIFA 是世界几大重要动画节的授权单位。官方网址：www.asifa.net。

3. ***Conceited General***《骄傲的将军》：上海美术电影制片厂 1956 年推出的动画作品，漫画家华君武担任编剧，特伟和李克弱担任导演。艺术家赴北京、山东、河北等地搜集古代绘画、雕塑、建筑等资料，经过一年多时间的辛勤工作完成了这部 20 多分钟的动画片。此片开创了中国民族风格动画片的先河，在中国动画史上占有重要的地位。

4. **shadow puppetry** 皮影戏

5. **Hu Jinqing** 胡进庆：中国美术片导演，1936 年生于江苏常熟，擅长剪纸。1953 年毕业于北京电影学校后，到上海美术电影制片厂工作，参加过《鹬蚌相争》、《淘气的金丝猴》、《草人》等 30 多部影片的拍摄。胡进庆对剪纸动画片的发展有着较大贡献，和著名导演万古蟾共同创作了中国第一部剪纸动画片《猪八戒吃西瓜》。

6. ***Piggy (Zhu Bajie) Eats the Watermelon*** 《猪八戒吃西瓜》：1958 年上海美术电影制片厂出品的 15 分钟剪纸动画片，万古蟾导演。

7. **Qi Baishi** 齐白石**(1864—1957)**：湖南湘潭人，是我国 20 世纪著名画家和书法篆刻家。曾任北京国立艺专教授、中央美术学院名誉教授，被授予“人民艺术家”称号。

8. ***Where Is Mama?*** 《小蝌蚪找妈妈》：上海美术电影制片厂 1961 年出品的水墨动画片。影片根据同名童话改编，取材于画家齐白石创作的鱼虾等形象。特伟担任艺术指导，钱家骏技术指导，段孝萱摄影。影片获第一届百花奖最佳美术片奖；瑞士第十四届洛迦诺国际电影节(Locarno)短片银帆奖；法国第四届昂西国际动画节(Annecy)短片特别奖；第四届法国戛纳国际电影节(Cannes)荣誉奖；第三届萨格勒布国际动画电影节(Zagreb)一等奖。

9. **Annecy** 法国昂西国际动画节：始创于 1960 年，是国际著名的动画节，在动画短片、动画长片、电视作品、学生毕业作品等领域设置不同奖项。官方网址：www. annecy.org。

10. **Cannes** 戛纳国际电影节(**Festival De Cannes**)：国际上规模最大、最重要的电影节之一，于 1946 年在法国南部旅游胜地戛纳举办了首届电影节，1957 年起设“金棕榈奖”，分别授予最佳故事片、纪录片、科教片、动画片等。

11. **Locarno** 洛迦诺国际电影节(**Locarno International Film Festival**)：1946 年创办于瑞士，是世界上最古老的国际电影节之一，它和戛纳、威尼斯、柏林并称“欧洲四大电影节”，素有“电影节中的王子”的美誉。

12. ***Buffalo Boy and the Flute*** 《牧笛》：上海美术电影制片厂 1963 年出品的水墨动画片，片长 20 分钟，特伟、钱家骏导演。本片于 1979 年获丹麦第三届欧登塞国际童话电影节(Odense International Fairy Tale Film Festival)金质奖。

13. ***Feelings from Mountain and Water*** 《山水情》：1988 年由上海美术电影制片厂拍摄的水墨动画片。片长 19 分钟，由王树忱编剧，特伟担任总导演，阎善春、马克宣导演，画家吴山明担任人物设计，山水画家卓鹤君担任背景设计，段孝萱担任水墨工艺设计兼摄影，金复载作曲，龚一古琴独奏。作品获第九届中国电影金鸡奖最佳美术片奖；苏联第一届莫斯科国际青少年电影节(Moscow International Youth Film Festival)“勇与美”奖；加拿大第十四届蒙特利尔国际电影节最佳短片奖等。此片是中国动画史中的一部艺术精品。

14. **Montreal International Film Festival** 加拿大蒙特利尔国际电影节：1977 年创办，电影节的主要目的是鼓励各国影坛的交流，促进各国电影事业的发展。

15. **Shanghai International Film Festivals** 上海国际电影节：创办于 1993 年，是中国国内第一个国际电影节，由国家广播电影电视总局和上海市政府主办，宗旨是：增进各国、各地区电影界人士之间的相互了解和友谊，促进世界电影艺术的繁荣。电影节共分为 4 个主要部分，包括评奖单元主竞赛单元金爵奖、国际电影交易市场，金爵国际电影论坛及国际电影展览放映。

16. **Shanghai Animation Film Studio** 上海美术电影制片厂：中国动画片创作的主要基地，前身是东北电影制片厂的卡通股，1949 年成立美术片组，次年迁到上海隶属上海电影制片厂。1957 年 4 月正式建厂，特伟为第一任厂长。上海美影厂在发展过程中汇集了一大批蜚声动画影坛的编剧、导演、美术设计师、摄影师、作曲家和技术专家。

17. **water and ink** 水墨：即水墨画，中国画的一种表现形式。一般指用水和墨为媒介的绘画艺术，由墨色的干、湿、浓、淡产生的丰富变化来表现物象，有着独特的艺术效果和民族美学价值。

18. **art films** 美术电影：是木偶片、剪纸片、水墨动画等中国动画片艺术形式的总称，主要运用绘画或其他造型形式来表现电影艺术家的创作意图。美术电影包括短片、长片和系列片等，题材和形式广泛多样，在世界影坛上占有重要地位。中国的美术电影从自己民族传统绘画、壁画、年画、雕刻、民间工艺和地方戏曲等各个方面汲取丰富的养料，逐渐形成了一种独特的动画艺术风格。

19. ***Lotus Lantern*** 《宝莲灯》：上海美术电影制片厂 1999 年出品的动画电影，常光希担任导演。

Comprehensive Questions

1. In what aspects did Te Wei try to combine his works with Chinese national styles?
2. What do you think made *Where Is Mama?* so successful?
3. Talk about Te Wei's three major achievements.
4. What do you think is the magic of water and ink films?
5. Te Wei believed that nationality should be preserved in doing animation. What do you think?

Further Reading

◎***Animation in Asia and the Pacific***

Author：John A. Lent

Publisher：Indiana University Press (2001)

◎***Created in China: The Great New Leap Forward***

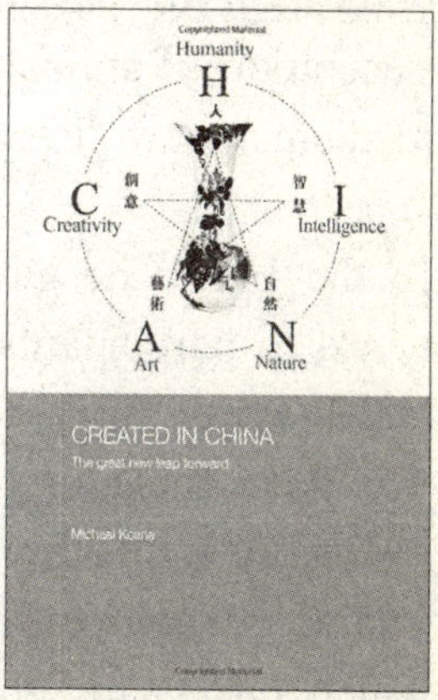

Author: Michael Keane

Publisher: Routledge (2007)

Web Links

www.ani-sh.com

11 CHAPTER

Text

Richard Williams and *The Animator's Survival Kit*[1]

Richard Williams[2] has a creative mind in the animation of the worldwide smash success ***Who Framed Roger Rabbit***[3]. He has won 3 Oscars, 3 **British Academy Awards**[4] and over 250 other international awards.

More than 50 years in the business, Williams has been one of the true innovators and serves as the link between the Golden Age of animation by hand and the new computer animation successes. Perhaps even more important is his dedication to passing along his knowledge to a new generation of animators so that they in turn can push the medium in new directions.

In the 1990's he gave the Richard Williams' Animation Masterclasses around the world to participants from studios such as Disney, Pixar, **ILM**[5], Dreamworks/**PDI**[6] and **Warner Bros**[7] followed by the best-selling *The Animators Survival Kit* (2001). The book includes techniques, advice, tips, tricks, and general information on the history of animation. The book is helpful for several fields of animation, not just traditional animation. Richard Williams' current project is a 16-DVD boxed set which brings together his legendary Masterclasses with his best-selling book to create *The Animator Survival Kit* Animated.

Praise for Richard Williams

"Arguably the best animator working in the field today."

—Hollywood Reporter

"Richard is a genius."

—Robert Zemeckis (director, Back to the Future, Who Framed Roger Rabbit, Forrest Gump)

"Probably one of the most respected draftsmen in the world."

—Los Angeles TV Times

"Williams is miles ahead of anyone in the world of animation."

—New York Times

"Voted by peers as 'The Animator's Animator'."

—Observer

EXTREMES and BREAKDOWNS(from the book)

Take the example of a swinging pendulum: The extremes are where there is a change in direction - the ends of the action where the direction changes.

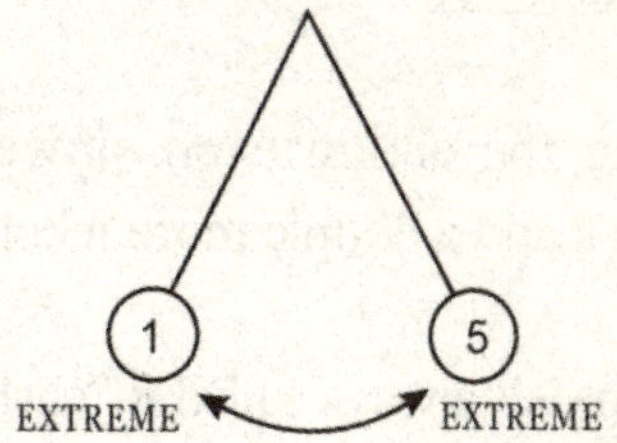

Because the pendulum's arm maintains its length as it swings, the middle position creates an arc in the action. We can see how important that middle position between the two extremes is going to be to us.

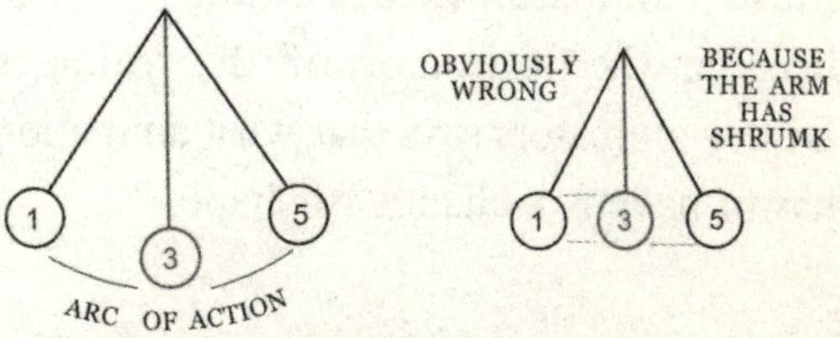

It's obvious how important this middle position is. In the 1930s they called this the '**breakdown**[8]' drawing or '**passing position**[9]' between two extremes.

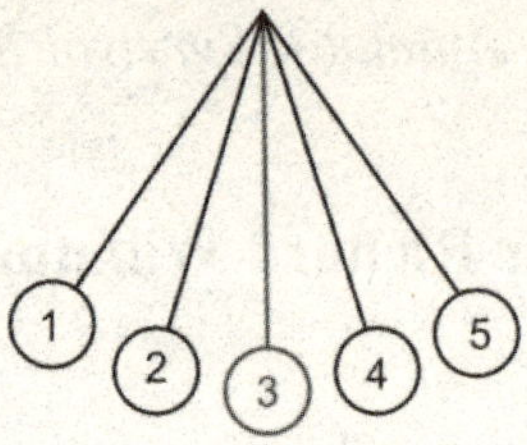

We'll add two **inbetweens**[10].

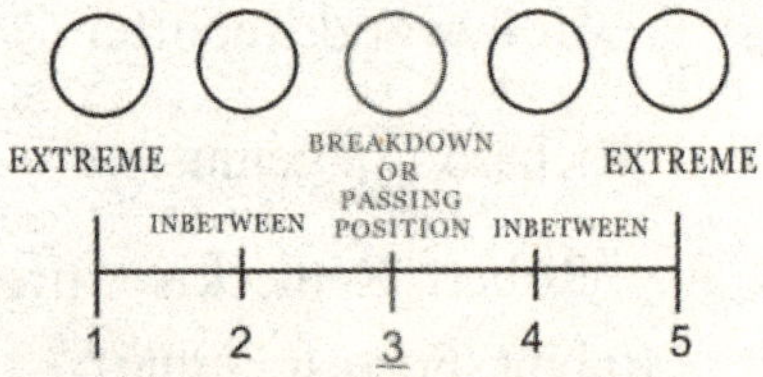

Some animations underline the breakdown or passing position because it's so important to the action. I have the habit of doing this because it's a position which is crucial to helping us invent. We're going to make tremendous use of this middle position later…

If we want to make our pendulum ease in and out of the extreme positions, we'll need a couple more inbetweens:

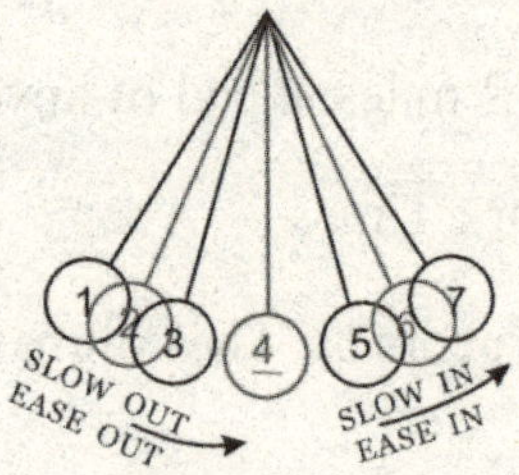

So our chart will look like this.

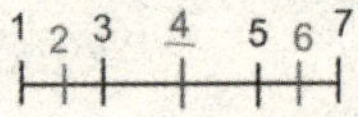

What we're doing is easing in or easing out of the extreme positions. 'Slowing in' or 'slowing out' is the classical terminology for it, but I prefer today's computer animators' term of 'easing in' and 'easing out'.

To make the action even slower at the ends, let's add a couple more inbetweens.

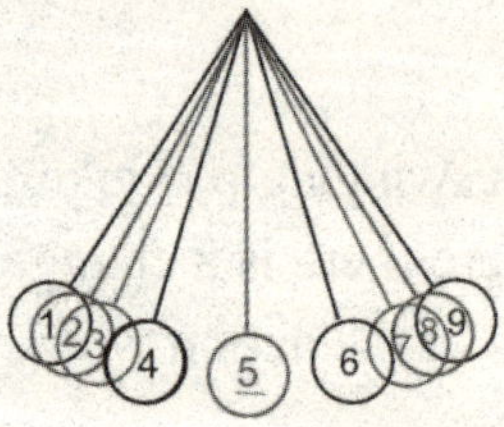

Now our chart will look like this.

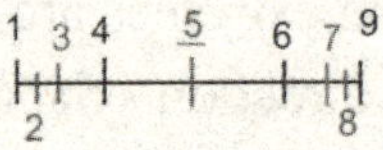

Ken Harris[11] always called it "cushioning"- which is a nice way to think of it. Master animator **Eric Larson**[12] – who became the instructor of the younger Disney animators says that what animation has to have is a change of shape.

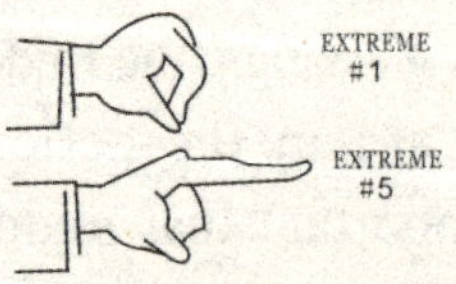

So, let's change from a closed hand to a pointing finger.

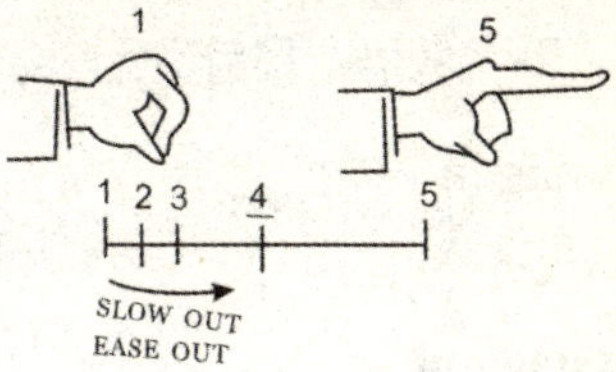

If we 'ease out' of number 1 in order to point – number5 - the chart will be:

Alternatively, if we '<u>snap out</u>' or 'speed out' of the closed hand and "ease in" or "cushion in" to the pointing finger the chart will be:

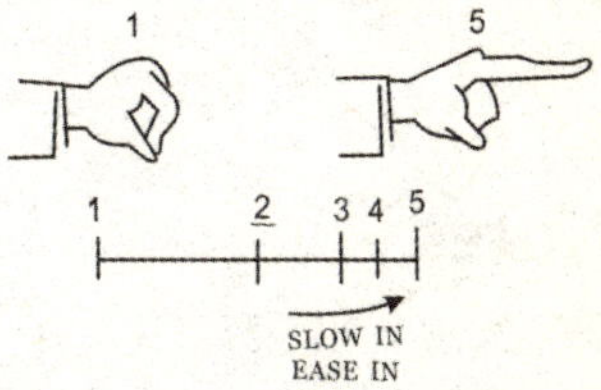

For a more relaxed, slower action we could add more inbetweens and ease out of the closed hand, and speed through the middle, and then ease in to the pointing finger.

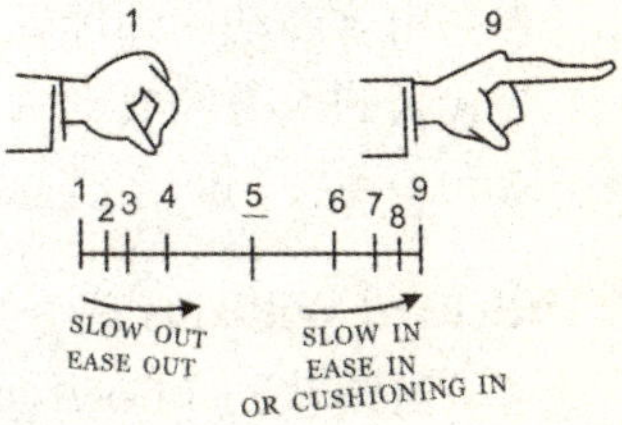

The animator can get away with just drawing the two extreme positions and making a chart for the assistant to put in all the inbetween positions.

Words and Phrases

smash [smæʃ]
adj. 了不起的；非常轰动的；出色的

innovator ['inəuveitə]
n. 改革者，创新者

serves as
担任，充当

dedication [,dedi'keiʃən]
n. 奉献；献身

in turn
转而

pendulum ['pendjuləm]
n. 钟摆；摇锤

extreme [ik'stri:m]
n. 极端；末端

arc [ɑ:k]
n. 弧度；圆弧

obvious ['ɔbviəs]
adj. 明显的；显著的

crucial ['kru:ʃəl]
adj. 重要的；决定性的

slowing in
慢入

slowing out
慢出

terminology [ˌtəːmiˈnɔlədʒi]
n. 术语；用辞

easing in
渐入

easing out
渐出

cushioning [ˈkuʃəniŋ]
n. 缓冲

snap out
快速脱离

Notes

1. ***The Animator's Survival Kit***《动画师生存手册》：Faber & Faber 出版社于 2001 年出版，本书由著名动画师理查德 · 威廉姆斯(Richard Williams)编著，全书深入讲解了以迪士尼为代表的西方经典动画的创作原则、制作规律及表现技巧，是迪士尼动画几十年制作经验和表现技巧的系统总结。

2. **Richard Williams** 理查德 · 威廉姆斯：迪士尼著名动画导演。曾以改编自狄更斯名著的《圣诞颂歌》(*A Christmas Carol*)获奥斯卡奖。其他著名作品有《谁害了兔子罗杰》(*Who Framed Roger Rabbit*)等片，著有《动画师生存手册》(*The Animator's Survival Kit*)一书 。

3. ***Who Framed Roger Rabbit***《谁害了兔子罗杰》：迪士尼 1988 年出品的真人与动画角色结合的电影，影片以 20 世纪 40 年代好莱坞黄金时期的动画王国为故事背景，片中出现了包括兔八哥、米老鼠、唐老鸭、贝蒂·布鲁等著名动画形象。由理查德·威廉姆斯 Richard Williams 担任动画导演。塑造了罗杰(Roger)、杰西卡(Jessica)等许多经典形象。

4. **British Academy Awards** 英国电影学院奖：由英国电影与电视艺术学会(British Academy of Film and Television Arts)举办。1947 年开始评奖，每年一次。设最佳影片、最佳英国影片、最佳纪录片、最佳专题片、最佳动画片等奖项。官方网址：www.bafta.org/awards 参见 Chapter9-21。

5. **ILM (industrial light and magic)** 工业光魔公司：1981 年由著名导演乔治·卢卡斯创立，是目前全球第一大特效制作公司。

6. **PDI (Pacific digital image)** 太平洋数码影像公司：是跟皮克斯(Pixar)同时代诞生的公司，后并入梦工厂(DreamWorks)。

7. **Warner Bros.** 华纳兄弟娱乐公司 **(Warner Bros. Entertainment, Inc.)**：简称华纳兄弟(Warner Bros.)，全球最大的电影和电视娱乐制作公司，是时代华纳(Time Warner)旗下子公司，总部分别位于美国加州的伯班克(Burbank)以及纽约市。在动画领域塑造了许多脍炙人口的作品。2010 年的最新电影《猫头鹰王国：守卫者传奇》(Legend of the Guardians: The Owls of Ga'Hoole)由扎克·施奈德 (Zack Snyder)导演。

8. **breakdown** 受控制帧：参见 Chapter2-22。

9. **passing position** 过渡位置

10. **Inbetween** 中间画

11. **Ken Harris** 肯·哈里斯 **(1898—1982)**：美国早期动画师，曾经在华纳、迪士尼、米高梅等许多工作室工作过，对美国早期动画的发展起到重要。他最成功的作品是在杰克·琼斯(Chuck Jones)旗下工作时完成的。

12. **Eric Larson** 艾瑞克·拉尔森**(1905—1988)**：美国早期著名的动画师，“迪士尼九老”之一。从 1933 年开始一直为迪士尼工作，参与的有《白雪公主》(*Snow White*)、《幻想曲》(*Fantasia*)《小鹿斑比》(*Bambi*)、《睡美人》(*Sleeping Beauty*)、《森林王子》(*The Jungle Book*)等著名动画作品。

Comprehensive Questions

1. How do you feel about Who Framed Roger Rabbit?
2. Try to illustrate the “extremes and breakdown principle” with more examples.

Further Reading

◎ ***The Animator's Survival Kit***

Author：Richard Williams

Publisher：Faber & Faber(2001)

Web Links

www.theanimatorssurvivalkit.com

12 CHAPTER

Text

Movie Gallery: *Up*

It is really hard to select the best **Pixar**[1] film. Everyone has different criteria. The ***Toy Stories***[2] and ***A Bug's Life***[3] are the beginning of it's productions which were fun and weren't like anyone we'd seen before. ***Finding Nemo***[4] was so moving and took the studio to new heights of popularity. ***The Incredibles***[5] was the most exciting thing they'd ever done. ***Cars***[6] made us feel both warm and nostalgic. ***Ratatouille***[7] was so classic. And *WALL-E* was so unique. If we're picking up our favorite Pixar film, that is easy for me: ***Monsters Inc***[8]**. Pete Docter's**[9] first film has all these qualities and is easy to be the funniest and most re-watchable. One docter does it again in *Up* — a fun, moving, exciting, nostalgic, classic and unique film!

Carl Fredricksen promised his bride a life of adventure. Instead they live a much more ordinary, but still happy life after marriage. When Carl is about to move forcibly from the house he and his wife lived in for decades, he makes a decision to start that adventure by getting himself and his beloved home both away from it. However, a stow-away, a rare bird, and a fallen hero make things much more adventurous than he had planned.

The first 10 minutes or so of *Up* might be the best animated moment ever put on screen — heart warming and wrenching at the same time. Pixar always says they develop a new technology for each film to help them achieve some effect (e.g. **Sully's fur**[10] and Nemo's watery world). *WALL-E* must have given the creative team a similar lift because the fact that almost all of those first 10 minutes of *Up* are done without dialogue makes all the feat more remarkable. Compared with any other Pixar films, *Up* is first and foremost a fantasy film. And since it takes place in our human world the leap to suspending disbelief has to be done right or everything else will seem natural. Luckily this is not an issue; either because of the skill of the writers or maybe because of the marketing of the film in which a good preparation was made for what the audience were going to see — whatever the reason it mostly works. Once you've gotten enjoying the first a few amazing minutes and then been introduced to the more fantastical elements of the film, everything else flows naturally.

The laughs come often and, unlike films from other studios, *Up* doesn't rely on pop culture references or inappropriate jokes that will hopefully go over the kids' heads. The humor of the film may surpass everything else Pixar has done before. But *Up*'s real center is its heart. And that is carried by its lead: an old man named Carl. Pixar has perhaps created a most sympathetic and trustworthy character in Carl. What he feels about every emotion is just what the audience feel. Making the viewers care so much about a character that most Hollywood types would never want cast as a lead in their film (live action or otherwise) could not have been an easy job but it seems effortless on the screen. The writers of *Up* have really surpassed themselves on humor, story and character development.

Up may be the most beautiful film in the Pixar vault. That may not be fair to the other films since this one features **South American waterfalls and tepuis**[11], and thousands of colorful balloons — what could compete with that! Most of the character designs may not have been the most original, but they were entirely serviceable. Carl himself is the best of the cast. From his curmudgeonly mien to his plodding gait, the design helps complete the lifelike image which absorbs the audience.

After outings like ***Lost***[12], *The Incredibles*, and ***Star Trek***[13], **Michael Giacchino**[14] is obviously my new favorite Hollywood composer. He delivers again in *Up* and shows his versatility with a score different from what he's done before but with a flair or style that still feels like the rest. From old-timey and quaint to emotive and poignant adventure — Giacchino easily slips between each aspect of the script and perfectly matches the tone with music.

Besides their story-telling prowess, perhaps the thing that sets Pixar apart from everyone else is their ability to match a voice to a character. Not just contented to find the most popular star of the moment to help their box office clout, they find the right voice for the job regardless of any other concern. **Ed Asner**[15] is not strange to voice acting for animation. But he gave the performance of his voice over career in this film. Some might even say it was one of his best performances in any venue. Asner is the third and maybe most important prong that brought this character to life. **Jordan Nagai**[16], as the wilderness scout Russell, seems a little stiff but whether that was an acting problem or a character decision is open to question. Either way using a "real kid" gave the role a more genuine quality than if a leading child actor had been hired to "act" the part. **Christopher Plummer**[17] as the villain is more than up to the part. And **co-director**[18] and writer **Bob Peterson**[19] prove the spirit of **Joe Ranft**[20] (voice of Heimlich and co-writer of A Bug's Life) alive on at Pixar in his hysterical performance as the talking dogs Dug and Alpha.

Director Pete Docter proves he is the king of comedy at Pixar with the studio's two funniest movies under his name. And Pixar continues to prove they are the best by what they do in the world right now — with great stories, superb animation, and lifelike characters. It'll be hard for any other animations to top *Up* this year.

Words and Phrases

criteria [krai'tiəriə]
n. 标准；条件

re-watchable [re-wɔtʒəbl]
adj. 值得反复观看的

nostalgic [nɔ'stældʒik]
adj. 对往事怀恋的，怀旧的

stow-away
逃票乘船、飞机等交通工具

wrench [rentʃ]
vt. 使…感到痛苦，使…难过

first and foremost
最重要的是，首要的是

suspend [sə'spend]
v. 把…搁置在一边

pop culture
n. 波普文化，通俗文化

sympathetic [ˌsimpə'θetik]
adj. 同情的

cast [kɑ:s, kæst]
vt. 分配角色

be fair to
对…公平

curmudgeonly [kə:'mʌdʒənli]
adj. 坏脾气的

mien [mi:n]
n. 仪表，神态，风采

plodding ['plɔdiŋ]
adj. 沉重缓慢的，单调乏味的

versatility [ˌvə:sə'tiliti] [ˌvɔsə'tiləti]
n. 多才多艺；用途广泛

flair [flɛə]
n. 天赋，才能

old-timey
adj. 旧时的，古色古香的；激起怀旧情怀的

quaint [kweint]
adj. 古色古香的

emotive [i'məutiv]
adj. 激起强烈感情的

poignant ['pɔinjənt, 'pɔignənt]
adj. 深刻的；深深打动人的

prowess ['prauis]
n. 高超的技艺，非凡的才能

of the moment
adv. 此刻

venue ['venju:]
n. 立场

prong [prɔg, prɔ:ŋ]
n. 分支，小队，小组

Notes

1. **Pixar Animation Studios** 皮克斯动画工作室：专门制作电脑动画的公司，由史蒂夫· 乔布斯(Steve Jobs)创立于 1986 年，其前身则是乔治· 卢卡斯(George Lucas)电影公司的电脑动画部。2006 年被迪士尼收购。除了制作动画影片外，皮克斯公司制定了三维软件渲染器规范 RenderMan，并开发出符合 RenderMan 规范的三维软件渲染器 PhotoRealistic RenderMan(简称 PRMan)，可以为绝大多数流行三维软件提供渲染服务。

2. ***Toy Stories*** 《玩具总动员》：动画系列电影，至今共制作了三部，由华特 · 迪士尼影片公司和皮克斯动画工作室合作推出。《玩具总动员》首部完全以 3D 电脑动画摄制而成的长篇剧情动画片，于 1995 年 11 月 22 日在北美公映；《玩具总动员 2》是皮克斯的首

部续集影片，于 1999 年 11 月 24 日在北美首映；《玩具总动员 3》是皮克斯的首部 IMAX 影片，于 2010 年 6 月 18 日在北美上映。

3. ***Finding Nemo*** 《海底总动员》：由皮克斯动画工作室制作，2003 年由迪士尼发行的美国电脑动画电影，是迪士尼和皮克斯合作的第五部长篇动画电影。

4. ***A Bug's Life*** 《虫虫特工队》：是迪士尼和皮克斯合作的第二部长篇动画电影，该片于 1998 年在北美上映，全球票房为 3.62 亿美元，成为当年动画长片票房冠军。

5. ***The Incredibles*** 《超人总动员》：是 2004 年皮克斯制作的三维动画电影，由布拉德• 伯德(Brad Bird)执导。这是迪士尼与皮克斯合作的第六部动画长片。获第 77 届奥斯卡最佳动画片奖。

6. ***Cars*** 《汽车总动员》：迪士尼和皮克斯合作的第七部长篇动画电影，是皮克斯公司成立 20 周年的纪念之作。 影片制作期间，迪士尼公司正式收购皮克斯， 该片也成为两家公司旧有合约下的最后一部电影。

7. ***Ratatouille*** 《美食总动员》：又译为《料理鼠王》，片名“Ratatouille”来自一款同名法国菜式，该片是皮克斯动画工作室被迪士尼收购后出品的第一部动画电影，全球票房超过 5 亿美元。

8. ***Monsters Inc.*** 《怪物公司》：是迪士尼和皮克斯合作的第四部长篇动画电影，也是迪士尼自创建以来首次起用“反派怪物”担当主角。

9. **Pete Docter** 彼得 · 道格特：《飞屋环游记》编剧、导演、配音，1990 年 5 月加入皮克斯动画工作室开始动画制作，除《飞屋环游记》外还曾在皮克斯制作的多部动画片中担任编剧、导演和配音工作，现为皮克斯制作团队中最重量级的人才之一。

10. **Sully's fur** 皮克斯旗下的创作团队在《怪物公司》的制作过程使用了具有新技术的动力学模拟，开创了震惊动画界的毛发渲染技术。Sully 的毛发的建模、渲染和变形是《怪物公司》在制作期间面临的最大技术挑战之一，这一技术难题地成功解决让皮克斯在动画界名声更加响亮。

11. **South American waterfalls and tepuis** 南美洲(委内瑞拉)的瀑布和平顶山区，《飞屋环游记》中的仙境瀑布及其周边地形的原形在委内瑞拉的天使瀑布一带，天使瀑布是世界上最高的瀑布。

12. ***Lost*** 电视剧《迷失》：美国 ABC 电视台斥巨资于夏威夷拍摄，是黄金时段收视率最高的电视剧之一，曾获 2005 年艾美奖最佳剧情类电视剧和 2006 金球奖剧情类最佳电视剧。

13. ***Star Trek*** 《星际旅行》：一部美国科幻娱乐电视剧系列，最早的《初代》于 1966 在美国全国广播公司(NBC)首播，其后衍生推出大量的电视剧集和电影，该系列产生了一群拥护剧中观念的狂热支持者，并慢慢融入了美国大多数人的文化当中。

14. **Michael Giacchino** 迈克 · 吉亚奇诺：美国作曲家，主要从事影视音乐创作，由其担纲音乐创作的《飞屋环游记》曾获第 67 届美国电影电视金球奖最佳原创配乐奖和第 82 届奥斯卡金像奖最佳配乐奖。

15. **Ed Asner** 爱德华 ·阿斯纳：美国电影、电视演员，在《飞屋环游记》中为 Carl Fredricksen 配音。

16. **Jordan Nagai** 乔丹 · 纳盖：《飞屋环游记》中 Russell 的配音演员。

17. **Christopher Plummer** 克里斯托弗 · 普卢默：加拿大演员，1927 年 12 月 13 日生于多伦多市，是一位舞台剧出身的演员，1965 年凭借电影《音乐之声》一举成名。

18. **co-director** 联合导演：由两名以上导演共同负责完成一部影片的摄制工作，联合导演的影片必须有一个执行导演，以保证摄制工作的顺利进行。

19. **Bob Peterson** 鲍勃 · 彼德森：《飞屋环游记》联合导演、编剧，自 1994 年以来就已在皮克斯动画工作室发挥了关键作用，除了从事故事创作工作之外，彼德森还经常为动画人物配音。

20. **Joe Ranft** 乔 · 兰福特：《虫虫特工队》中 Heimlich 的配音演员。

Comprehensive Questions

1. What is special about the first 10 minutes of Up?
2. What is special about the humor of Up?
3. How you understand the “real center” of Up?
4. The success of Up proves that a good work is usually the combination of many elements. Give one or two other films to illustrate this point.

Further Reading

◎ ***To Infinity and Beyond!: The Story of Pixar Animation Studios***

Author: Karen Paik

Publisher: Chronicle Books (2007)

◎ ***The Pixar Touch***

Author: David A. Price

Publisher: Vintage (2009)

Web Links

www.animatedviews.com

www.animationmagazine.net

Part 3

拓展篇

Animation English Course

13 CHAPTER

Text

Computer Animation Technology (1)

Computer animation is the process to generate animated images by using computer graphics. The general term **computer generated imagery(CGI)**[1] encompasses both static scenes and dynamic images, while computer animation only refers to moving images produced by exploiting the **persistence of vision**[2] to make a series of images look animated. Given that images last for about one twenty-fourth second on the **retina**[3], fast image replacement creates the illusion of movement.

Modern computer animation usually uses **3D computer graphics**[4], although **2D computer graphics**[5] are still used for stylistic, low **bandwidth**[6], and faster real-time renderings. Sometimes the target of the animation is the computer itself, but sometimes the target is another medium, such as film.

Computer animation is essentially a digital successor to the art of stop motion animation of 3D models and frame-by-frame animation of 2D illustrations. To create the illusion of movement, an image is displayed on the computer screen and repeatedly replaced by a new image that is similar to the previous image, but advanced slightly in the **time domain**[7] (usually at a rate of 24 or 30 frames/second). This technique is identical to how the illusion of movement is achieved with television and motion pictures.

For 3D animations, objects (models) are built on the computer monitor and 3D figures are rigged with a virtual skeleton. For 2D figure animations, separate objects (illustrations) and separate transparent layers are used, with or without a virtual skeleton. Then the figures limbs, eyes, mouth, clothes, etc. are moved by the animator on **key frames**[8]. The differences in appearance between key frames are automatically calculated by the computer in a process known as **tweening**[9] or **morphing**[10]. Finally, the animation is rendered.

For 3D animations, all frames must be rendered after modeling is complete. For 2D **vector**[11] animations, the rendering process is the key frame illustration process, while **tweened frames**[12] are rendered as needed. For pre-recorded presentations, the rendered frames are transferred to a different format or medium such as film or digital video. The frames may also be rendered in real time as they are presented to the end-user audience. Low bandwidth animations transmitted via the internet (e.g. **2D Flash**[13], **X3D**[14]) often use software on the end-user's computer to render in real time as an alternative to **streaming** [15] or pre-loaded high bandwidth animations.

History

CGI was initially used in the movie ***Westworld***[16](1973), a science-fiction film about a society in which robots live and work among humans. Though the first use of **3D Wireframe imagery**[17] was in its sequel, ***Futureworld***[18] (1976), which featured a computer-generated hand and face was created by University of Utah graduate students **Edwin Catmull**[19] and **Fred Parke**[20]. The third movie to use this technology was ***Star Wars***[21] (1977). ***The Black Hole***[22] (1979) used raster **wire-frame**[23] model rendering to depict a black hole. That year the science fiction-horror film ***Alien***[24] also used a raster wire-frame model, in this case to render the image of navigation monitors in the sequence where a spaceship follows a beacon to a land on an unfamiliar planet.

In 1978, graduate students at the **New York Institute of Technology Computer Graphics Lab**[25] began to work on what would have been the first full-length CGI film, The Works, and a trailer for it was shown at 1982's **SIGGRAPH**[26], but the film was never completed. ***Star Trek II: The Wrath of Khan***[27] premiered a short CGI sequence called *The Genesis Wave* in June, 1982. The first two films made a heavy investments in Solid 3D CGI, ***Tron***[28] (1982) and ***The Last Starfighter***[29] (1984), were commercial failures, causing most directors to relegate CGI to images that were supposed to look like they were created by a computer. Another Star Trek movie - 1986's ***Star Trek IV: The Voyage Home***[30] - features a little-known use of CGI that would prove to be a major stepping stone for the technology in years to come.

The first movie to feature photo-realistic CGI integrated seamlessly into scenes was ***The Abyss***[31] (1989). A five-minute sequence featuring an animated water tentacle or "pseudopod" was created through using groundbreaking new **algorithms**[32] design by **ILM**[33], and supervised by **Denis Muren**[34] for **James Cameron's**[35] underwater action movie.

Words and Phrases

general term
通用术语，常用术语；总称

encompass [in'kʌmpəs]
vt. 包含；包围，环绕；完成

refer to
指，指代；涉及；引用

a series of
一系列的；一连串的

last [lɑ:st, læst]
持续；延续；历时…

target ['tɑ:git]
n. 目标；靶子

successor [sək'sesə]
n. 继承者；后续的事物

previous ['pri:vjəs]
adj. 以前的；早先的

be identical to
与…相同

monitor ['mɔnitə]
n. 显示器

rig [rig]
v. 操纵，控制

skeleton ['skelitən]
n. 骨架，骨骼；纲要

real time
实时

be presented to
呈现给

end-user ['end,ju:zə]
n. 计算机终端用户

science-fiction
科幻的

sequel ['si:kwel]
n. 续集；结局

navigation monitor
向导监视窗口

beacon ['bi:kən]
n. 灯塔，指路明灯

investment in
对…的投资；在…方面的投资

prove to be
结果是，证明为

stepping stone
垫脚石；跳板

photo-realistic
真实感图形，照相写实主义的

seamlessly ['si:mlisli]
adv. 无缝地

tentacle ['tentəkl]
n. 触手，触须，触角

pseudopod ['psju:dəpɔd]
n. 动植物的伪足，假足

groundbreaking ['graund,breikiŋ]
adj. 开创性的

Notes

1. **computer generated imagery(CGI)** 电脑影像合成技术：是计算机数字图像(Computer Graphics，简称 CG)在影视特技领域的应用。

2. **persistence of vision** 视觉暂留现象：是指物体在快速运动时，当人眼所看到的影像消失后，人眼在一小段时间内仍能继续保留其影像，这个时间值是大约是 0.1 到 0.4 秒。视觉暂留现象是动画、电影等视觉媒体形成和传播的最基本的原理。

3. **retina** 视网膜：眼球最内层的薄膜。人眼观看物体时，成像于视网膜上，并由视神经输入人脑，感觉到物体的像。

4. **3D computer graphics(3D CG)** 三维计算机图形：是计算机和特殊三维软件帮助下创造的艺术作品。在动画领域，3D CG 常常被用来指代三维动画相关艺术作品。

5. **2D computer graphics(2D CG)** 二维计算机图形：是基于二维技术产生的计算机数字图像艺术。在动画领域，有时 2D CG 也特指利用计算机进行的二维动画创作或者常说的“无纸动画”。2D CG 的应用领域并不限于在二维动画，有很多三维动画作品中的背景、贴图都需要用到 2D CG 来创作。

6. **low bandwidth** 低带宽：带宽通常表示一个网络或者数据传输媒体携带的数据的容量。它表示在单位时间内从一点到另一点能够传递的最大数据量。

7. **time domain** 时间域：这里指小于视觉暂留时间的一小段时间，在动画中通常是 1/24 或者 1/30 秒。在这段时间内，计算机动画完成动画稿的替换，使得画稿上的动画形象看起来是运动的。

8. **key frames** 关键帧：帧就是动画中的单幅画面，相当于电影胶片上的每一格镜头。关键帧相当于传统手绘动画中的原画，指角色或者物体运动变化中的关键画面。由于计算机动画可以完成一部分过渡帧或者中间帧，使动画的制作得到了简化。

9. **tweening** 补间动画：在基于关键帧的动画制作法中，动画师先做好关键帧，然后由此再制作出其他中间帧，这也是计算机动画所采用的基本原理。由计算机自动运算并补齐的中间帧动画，也称为“补间动画”。

10. **Morphing** 形变动画：简单地说就是由一种形状变形为另一种形状的动画。它可以是二维动画中简单的由正方形变为圆形动画，或者是三维动画中立方体变为球体的动画；也可以是利用 anime studio 或者三维动画软件中的骨骼系统制作出的复杂的人物角色的动作变形动画。这种动画一般都是针对矢量对象的。

11. **vector** 矢量：计算机显示的图形一般分为两类——矢量图和位图。矢量图与分辨率无关可无限放大不失真。基于矢量图形制作的动画被称为矢量动画。

12. **tweened frames** 补间帧：在补间动画中，由计算机自动运算并补齐的中间帧。

13. **2D Flash**：Flash 是目前最受欢迎的二维矢量动画制作软件，在网页制作、多媒体、影视等领域都有着广泛应用。现如今 Flash 已经成为网络矢量动画的既定标准，被世界各地动画爱好者所热衷。

14. **X3D (Extensible 3D)** 可扩展 3D：是一个软件标准，定义了如何在多媒体中整合基于网络传播的交互三维内容。X3D 的发展有助于 3D 图形和动画等艺术作品的网络实时传播。

15. **Streaming** 流媒体：指对网络视频、动画等多媒体文件边下载边播放的流式传输方式。流媒体传输模式下，由视频服务器向用户计算机连续、实时传送数据，可实现边下载边观看。

16. ***Westworld*** 《西方世界》：又译作《钻石宫》，是 1973 年由著名科幻作家迈克尔 · 克莱顿(Michael Crichton)编导的科幻电影，是首部以二维计算机图形技术(2D CGI)为卖点的电影。影片的续集《未来世界》(*Futureworld*)则是首部应用三维计算机图形技术(3D CGI)的电影。

17. 3D Wireframe imagery 三维线框图像：指线框形式的三维模型图像，指代早期比较原始的、粗糙的三维计算机图形技术。

18. ***Futureworld***《未来世界》：又译作《翡翠窝大阴谋》，是《钻石宫》 (*Westworld*)的续集，于1976年在美国上映。由Richard T. Heffron导演，当年还是犹他大学研究生的艾德文 ·卡特姆(Edwin Catmull)和助理教授弗雷德里克 · 帕克(Fred Parke)用电脑制作了虚拟人物图像，使此片成为首部应用三维计算机图形技术(3D CGI)的电影。

19. Edwin Catmull 艾德文 · 卡特姆：1945 年 3 月生于美国西弗吉尼亚，是一个美国计算机科学家，皮克斯的创始人之一。20 世纪 70 年代末期，卡特姆开始致力于三维计算机图形学，并在 1979 年成为卢卡斯影业计算机图形学部门的副主管。1986 年，史提夫 ·乔布斯买下卢卡斯影业的计算机部门，成立了皮克斯，卡特姆担任首席技术官。

20. Fred Parke 弗雷德里克 · 帕克：毕业于美国犹他州大学，1974 年获得计算机博士学位，帕克制作了历史上第一个人脸三维计算机模型，该模型在 1976 年《未来世界》一片中使用。帕克现为美国德克萨斯州农工大学(Texas A&M University)建筑学院教授和可视化实验室主任。

21. ***Star Wars*** 《星球大战》：是美国导演乔治 · 卢卡斯所制作拍摄的一系列科幻电影。特效公司“工业光魔(ILM)”随影片一齐诞生，成为第一个具有划时代意义的特效电影公司。1977 版《星球大战》被认为开启了特效电影的一个数码科技新时代。

22. ***The Black Hole*** 《黑洞》：是迪士尼于 1979 年在美国推出的一部科幻惊悚片。该片运用了许多创新的电影特效，获得奥斯卡最佳特效奖提名。

23. wire-frame 线框建模：线框建模生成的实体模型是由一系列的直线、圆弧、点及自由曲线组成，描述的是物体的轮廓外形。线框建模的优点是所需信息最少，数据运算简单，所占存储空间较小，对硬件的要求不高。

24. ***Alien*** 《异形》：1979 年出品的科幻恐怖电影。

25. New York Institute of Technology Computer Graphics Lab 纽约理工学院计算机图形学实验室：是世界著名计算机图形学的研究和开发机构之一，三维电脑动画的诞生地。1974 年，卡特姆(Edwin Catmull)研究生毕业后担任实验室主管，并组建了一个动画研究小组，并集中精力开发协助动画师的工具软件。

26. SIGGRAPH 是由 ACM SIGGRAPH(美国计算机协会计算机图形专业组)组织的计算机图形学年度会议，第一届于 1974 年召开。

27. ***Star Trek II: The Wrath of Khan*** 《星际旅行 2：可汗之怒》：1982 年上映的《星舰迷航》系列的第二部电影，和 1977 年开始上映的《星球大战》系列，并称为国际两大科幻文化。

28. ***Tron***《电子世界争霸战》：1982 年由博伟影业公司(Buena Vista)发行。该片是第一部采用电脑成像(CGI)和真人结合的方式完成特效的电影，被认为是开创了 CG 制作电影的新纪元。

29. ***The Last Starfighter*** 《最后的星球斗士》：1984 年环球影片公司(Universal Picture)推出的科幻电影，是分形图形推向好莱坞影视业的应用影片之一(另一部典型应用是《星际旅行 2：可汗之怒》)。

30. ***Star Trek IV: The Voyage Home***《星际旅行 4：抢救未来》：1986 年上映的《星舰迷航》系列的第四部电影。

31. ***The Abyss***《深渊》：1989 年卡梅隆(James Cameron)自编自导的著名科幻影片，该片中大量的水下特技效果、计算机动画与实景片段合成成为该片的技术亮点。

32. algorithms 算法：是计算机解决某个问题的所需要的相对固定的套路和办法；或者说是为了让计算机完成某个任务，人们设计的相对机械的、统一的方法，这种方法可以很容易的转化为计算机程序。计算机算法是计算机程序的核心。

33. ILM (Industrial Light & Magic) 工业光学魔术公司：简称工业光魔，1981 年由著名导演乔治 · 卢卡斯创立，凭借《星球大战》开创了特效电影的新时代，目前是全球第一大特效制作公司，数次获得奥斯卡最佳视觉效果奖。有《侏罗纪公园》、《加勒比海盗》、《绿巨人》、《龙卷风》、《拯救大兵瑞恩》等著名影片。

34. Denis Muren 丹尼斯 · 穆伦：ILM 公司的视觉特效师，代表作有《世界大战》(2005)、《人工智能》(2001)等。

35. James Cameron 詹姆斯 · 卡梅隆：1954 年生于加拿大，擅长拍摄动作片以及科幻电影，执导了目前电影票房史上最卖座的两部电影《泰坦尼克号》(1997)和《阿凡达》(2009)。卡梅隆电影的主题往往试图探讨人和技术之间的关系。

Comprehensive Questions

1. How is the illusion of movement created in computer animation?
2. What is tweening?
3. How are *Star Trek IV: The Voyage Home* and *The Abyss* important?

Further Reading

◎***Essential Computer Animation : How to Understand the Techniques and Potential of Computer Animation***

Author：John Vince

Publisher: Springer (2000)

Web Links

www.cgsociety.org

14 CHAPTER

Text

Computer Animation Technology (2)

The year 1991 could be considered a breakout of the new CGI technology. Two huge hits, ***Terminator 2: Judgment Day***[1] and ***Beauty and the Beast***[2], both made good use of CGI. These successes marked Hollywood's transition from stop-motion animation and conventional **optical effects**[3] to digital techniques. *Beauty and the Beast* became the first animated film to be nominated as the Best Picture, and *Terminator 2: Judgment Day* won the Oscar for the Best Visual Effects.

In 1993, another affirmation of CGI came from ***Jurassic Park***[4] where CGI dinosaurs were integrated into **hydraulically-controlled**[5] life-sized puppets shot on-set. The palette of tools available from CGI become larger. In 1994, CGI was used for creating the special effects in **Forrest Gump**[6]. The most noteworthy effects shots were those that featured the digital removal of actor Gary Sinise's legs. Other effects included the fast-moving Ping-Pong balls, and the digital insertion of **Tom Hanks**[7] into several scenes of historical footage.

In 1995, the first fully computer-generated feature film, Disney-Pixar's *Toy Story*, was a resounding commercial success. Additional digital animation studios such as

Blue Sky Studios[8], **Sony Pictures Animation**[9] went into production, and existing animation companies, such as The Walt Disney Company, began to make a transition from traditional animation to CGI.

In the early 2000s, computer-generated imagery became the dominant form of special effects. **Camera tracking**[10] software was refined to gradually allow complex visual effects developments that were previously impossible. Virtual sets, in which part or all of the background of a shot is digitally generated, also became commonplace.

CGI for films is usually rendered at about 1.4–6 megapixels. *Toy Story*, for example, was rendered at 1536 × 922 (1.42MP). The time to render one frame is typically around 2–3 hours, with ten times that for the most complex scenes. The time has not changed much in the last decade. As image quality has progressed at the same rate as improvements in hardware, with faster machines, more and more complexity becomes feasible. Exponential increases in **GPUs**[11] processing power, as well as massive increases in parallel CPU power, storage and memory speed and size have greatly increased CGI's potential.

Developments of CGI technologies are reported each year at SIGGRAPH, an annual conference on computer graphics and interactive techniques, with tens of thousands of computer professionals attendence each year. Developers of computer games and 3D video cards strive to achieve the same visual quality on personal computers in real-time as is possible for CGI films and animation.

The future

For the moment it looks like three dimensional computer animation can be divided into two main directions: photorealistic and non-photorealistic rendering. Photorealistic computer animation can be itself divided into two subcategories: real photorealism (where **performance capture**[12] is used in the creation of the virtual human characters) and stylized photorealism. Real photorealism is what *Final Fantasy* tried to achieve and will be in the future

most likely to be able to give us live action fantasy features as ***The Dark Crystal***[13], while ***Antz***[14] is an example on stylistic photorealism. None of these mentioned above is perfected now, but the progress continues. The non-photorealistic/cartoonish direction is more like an extension of traditional animation, an attempt to make the animation look like a three dimensional version of a cartoon, still using and perfecting the main principles of animation articulated by the **Disney's Nine Old Men**[15], such as squash and stretch.

Words and Phrases

conventional [kən'venʃənəl]
adj. 符合习俗的，传统的；常见的；惯例的

be integrated into
与…相结合，统一到…中

dominant ['dɔminənt]
adj. 占优势的；支配的

commonplace ['kɔmənpleis]
n. 老生常谈；司空见惯的事；普通的东西

megapixel ['megə,piksəl]
n. 百万像素

feasible ['fi:zəbl]
adj. 可行的；可能的；可实行的

exponential [,ekspəu'nenʃəl]
adj. 指数的；*n.* 指数

processing power
处理能力

for the moment
暂时，暂且；目前

three dimensional
三维的；立体的

Notes

1. ***Terminator 2: Judgment Day***《终结者 2：审判日》：卡梅隆 1991 年编导的科幻影片，丹尼斯·穆伦(Denis Muren)担任视觉特效师。
2. ***Beauty and the Beast***《美女与野兽》：迪士尼公司 1991 年推出的动画片，是第一部获奥斯卡奖提名的动画长片。
3. **optical effects** 视觉效应：文中指代利用定格动画逐格拍摄手法和其他传统特效手段实现的视觉效果。

4. ***Jurassic Park*** 《侏罗纪公园》：1993 年环球影业公司推出的科幻电影，由史蒂文 · 斯皮尔伯格执导。1997 年拍摄续集《侏罗纪公园：失落的世界》(*The Lost World: Jurassic Park*)，2001 年拍摄第三集《侏罗纪公园 3》(*Jurassic Park III*)。片中使用了大量电脑影像合成技术(CGI)，为电影特效史上的里程碑。

5. **hydraulically-controlled** 液压控制装置：在传统电影特效制作方法中，有很多诸如地面晃动等特效需要利用这种装置来实现(在布景下面安装液压装置)。这里间接指代传统电影特效制作方法。

6. ***Forrest Gump*** 《阿甘正传》：是一部根据同名小说改编的美国电影，本片运用了大量的电脑合成特效来还原逼真的历史情景。

7. **Tom Hanks** 汤姆·汉克斯：美国影星，以演技精湛而著称，代表作有《阿甘正传》、《费城故事》、《西雅图不眠夜》、《拯救大兵瑞恩》、《达芬奇密码》等多部不同类型电影。他曾于 1994 年、1995 年连续两届荣获奥斯卡影帝，是好莱坞最具影响力的电影明星之一。

8. **Blue Sky Studios** 蓝天工作室：由克里斯 · 伟基(Chris Wedge)于 1987 年创建， 1998 年推出动画短片《兔子邦尼》，荣获第 71 届奥斯卡最佳动画短片奖。2002 年，福克斯公司(20th Century Fox Distribution)与蓝天工作室推出《冰河世纪》(Ice Age)系列，奠定了蓝天工作室在卡通片领域的地位。

9. **Sony Pictures Animation** 索尼影视动画公司：是索尼影视娱乐有限公司(Sony Pictures Entertainment SPE)的子公司，成立于 2002 年，主要为 SPE 开发制作所有电脑特效。公司的第一部故事片是发布于 2006 年的《丛林大反攻》(*Open Season*)，最新作品为 2009 年的《天降美食》(*Cloudy with a Chance of Meatballs*)。官方网址：www.sonypictures.com。

10. **camera tracking** 摄影机追踪：在科幻电影中，经常出现由计算机软件制作的虚拟角色活动于现实场景中，与真人同台"表演"，这就是利用摄影机追踪实现的特效。摄影机跟踪功能可能轻松地捕捉实拍时摄影机的运动轨迹，这样虚拟摄影机就可以将三维造型逼真地"放置"在实景中。

11. **GPUs (Graphic Processing Unit)** 图形处理器：是显卡上一个专门的负责图形处理的核心处理器。其最初目的是帮助 CPU 来进行图形的处理，这样一方面可以减轻 CPU 的负荷，另外一方面可以使图形更为逼真、速度更快。

12. **performance capture** 表演捕捉技术："表演捕捉"相比起传统的"动作捕捉"技术更进一步，可同时在录制过程中以三维特效的形式将多名演员的面部表情及肢体行为真实地再现出来，并通过完善的数字摄影系统提供全方位的拍摄信息。

13. ***The Dark Crystal*** 《夜魔水晶》：是 1982 年吉姆 · 汉森(Jim Henson)导演的一部风格偏黑暗的作品，由英国 ITC 娱乐公司(Incorporated Television Company)和美国吉姆 · 汉森制造公司(Jim Henson Productions)制作。

14. ***Antz*** 《蚁哥正传》：是 1998 年由梦工厂制作的三维动画电影，由埃里克 · 达尼尔(Eric Darnell)和蒂姆 · 约翰逊(Tim Johnson)执导。该片是继《玩具总动员》之后，美国第二部全电脑动画片。

15. Disney's Nine Old Men 迪士尼九大元老：是迪士尼公司开创时期的核心动画师(其中有些成为了导演)，他们创造了从《白雪公主》到《救难小英雄》(*The Rescuers Down Under*)时期最知名的动画长片。华特 · 迪士尼当时戏称这组动画师为他的九大元老，包括：Les Clark、Ollie Johnston、Frank Thomas、Wolfgang Reitherman (昵称 Woolie)、John Lounsbery、Eric Larson、Ward Kimball、Milt Kahl、Marc Davis。这九大元老创立了动画的 12 个基本准则(参见 Chapter5、6)。

Comprehensive Questions

1. Try to evaluate the transition from traditional animation to CGI.
2. If you are asked to add more to the history of CGI films, what films would you choose?
3. Explain the two major directions of photorealism and non-photorealism in 3D animation.

Further Reading

◎ ***The Art of 3D Computer Animation and Effects***

Author: Isaac Kerlow

Publisher: Wiley (2009)

Web Links

www.cgfocus.com

15 CHAPTER

Text

SIGGRAPH

In the span of 35 years, **ACM SIGGRAPH**[1] has grown from a handful of computer graphics enthusiasts to a diverse group of researchers, artists, developers, filmmakers, scientists, and other professionals who share an interest in **computer graphics**[2] and interactive techniques. Our community values excellence, passion, integrity, volunteerism, and **cross-disciplinary interaction**[3]. It sponsor not only the annual SIGGRAPH conference, but also focused symposia, **chapters**[4] in cities throughout the world, awards, grants, educational resources, online resources, a public policy program. ACM SIGGRAPH's parent organization is ACM, the Association for Computing Machinery.

ACM

ACM is the world's largest educational and scientific computing society, uniting educators, researchers, and professionals to inspire dialogue, share resources, and address the field's challenges. ACM strengthens the computing profession's collective voice through strong leadership, promotion of the highest standards, and recognition of technical excellence. ACM supports the professional growth of its members by providing opportunities for life-long learning, career development, and professional networking. Many ACM SIGGRAPH members also join ACM. The benefits of ACM membership include full access to online books and courses, the ACM Career & Job Center, subscriptions to ACM's popular email alert news digests TechNews and CareerNews, and the online newsletter Member-Net. ACM members may subscribe to the **Digital Library**[5] and receive full access to the **Guide to Computing Literature**[6], which features more than one million bibliographic citations from the vast world of computing.

AWARDS

ACM SIGGRAPH awards the prestigious **Steven A. Coons award**[7] for lifetime achievement, the **Computer Graphics Achievement Award**[8] for notable achievements, the **Significant New Researcher Award**[9] for new contributors to our field, the **Outstanding Service Award**[10] and **the Distinguished Artist Award**[11] for lifetime achievement in digital art.

DIGITAL ARTS COMMUNITY

The ACM SIGGRAPH Digital Arts Community committee serves to foster the evolution of a strong digital arts community within the international organization and to promote a dialogue between visual artists and the larger SIGGRAPH community. It maintains an interactive Arts Portal, arts.siggraph.org, with an associated social networking site, siggrapharts.ning.com that provides a central place for artists and scientists to share resources, information, artwork, and opportunities. All SIGGRAPH members are invited to utilize the site to follow developments in the arts, stay connected, and identify potential collaborators.

The Annual SIGGRAPH Conference

Some highlights of the conference are its **Animation Theater and Electronic Theater presentations**[12], where recently created CG films are played. There is a large exhibition floor, where several hundred companies set up elaborate booths and compete for attention and recruits. Most of the companies are in the engineering, graphics, motion picture, or video game industries. There are also many booths for schools which specialize in computer graphics or interactivity.

Dozens of research papers are presented each year, and SIGGRAPH is widely considered the most prestigious forum for the publication of computer graphics research. The recent paper acceptance rate for SIGGRAPH has been less than 20%. The papers accepted for presentation at SIGGRAPH are currently printed in a special issue of the ACM Transactions on Graphics journal. In addition to the papers, there are numerous panels of industry experts set up to discuss a wide variety of topics, from computer graphics to **machine interactivity**[13] to education. SIGGRAPH also offers many full- and half-day courses in state-of-the-art computer graphics topics.

In 1984, Pixar's first animated short, ***The Adventures of André & Wally B.***[14], premiered at SIGGRAPH. Pixar has debuted numerous shorts at the conference since.

The SIGGRAPH Asia Conference[15]

Since 2008, a second yearly SIGGRAPH conference has been held in Asia. The first SIGGRAPH Asia conference was held in Singapore from the tenth to the thirteenth of December 2008 at **the Suntec Singapore International Convention and Exhibition Centre**[16];the second one is held in Yokohama, Japan in the period from 16 December to 19 December, 2009 at **Pacifico Yokohama**[17]; and the third one is held in Seoul, Korea in the time period from 15 December to 18 December, 2010 at **COEX Convention & Exhibition Center Seoul**[18].and SIGGRAPH Asia 2011 will be in Hongkong in the period from 12 December to 15 December.

Words and Phrases

enthusiast [in'θju:ziæst]
n. 热衷于…的人；狂热者

volunteerism [ˌvɔlən'tiərizəm]
n. 志愿者精神；志愿者服务

sponsor ['spɔnsə]
vt. 赞助；发起

symposium [sim'pəuziəm]
n. 座谈会；专题讨论会

grant [grɑ:nt, grænt]
n. 拨款；授予物

inspire [in'spaiə]
vt. 激发，唤起

address [ə'dres]
vt. 从事；忙于

collective [kə'lektiv]
adj. 集体的；共同的

promotion [prəu'məuʃən]
n. 提升，促进；振兴

recognition [ˌrekəg'niʃən]
n. 识别；承认；赞誉

digest [di'dʒest, 'daidʒest]
n. 文摘；摘要

subscribe to
订阅

bibliographic [ˌbibliə'græfik]
adj. 书目的；书籍解题的

prestigious [pre'stidʒəs]
adj. 有名望的；享有声望的

foster ['fɔstə]
vt. 培养，促进，激励

portal ['pɔ:təl]
n. 网络出入口，门户站点

elaborate [i'læbərət, i'læbəreit]
adj. 精心制作的

booth [bu:ð, bu:θ]
n. 展位，展台

recruit [ri'kru:t]
n. 招聘；新成员

state-of-the-art
adj. 最先进的，达到最高水准的

Notes

1. **ACM SIGGRAPH**：ACM 全称 Association for Computing Machinery(美国计算机学会)；SIGGRAPH 全称 Special Interest Group on Computer Graphics(计算机图形学专业组)。ACM SIGGRAPH 特指由美国计算机学会组织的全球性质的计算机图形学年度会议，成立于 1967 年，致力于推广和发展计算机绘图和动画制作的软硬件技术。第一届 SIGGRAPH 会议于 1974 年召开。

2. **computer graphics(CG)** 计算机图形学：是研究怎样用数字计算机生成、处理和显示图形的一门学科。随着计算机图形学研究的深入，人们也开始习惯把计算机图形学及相关作品通称为CG。

3. **cross-disciplinary interaction** 跨学科互动

4. **ACM SIGGRAPH Chapters** ： ACM SIGGRAPH在世界各地拥有30多个专业分会以及8个面向学生的地方分会。北京设有ACM SIGGRAPH的专业分会。

5. **ACM Digital Library ACM** 数字图书馆 ：是ACM提供的期刊以及会议论文全文数据库，广泛地收录多种ACM电子出版物。

6. **Guide to Computing Literature (ACM)** 在线计算机文献指南：是ACM提供的文摘数据库，提供了超过3000家出版社在计算机领域出版的多种文献引文和摘要目录的查询和浏览功能，收录范围涉及图书、期刊、会议录、博士论文、技术报告等内容。

7. **Steven A. Coons Award** 考恩斯奖：是ACM SIGGRAPH早在1983年为纪念考恩斯而设立以他的名字命名的奖项。考恩斯为计算机图形学的先驱，曾提出现在在计算机动画中广泛使用的B样条曲面、NURB表面等几何模型的数学基础。

8. **Computer Graphics Achievement Award** 计算机图形学成就奖：该奖项主要颁发给在计算机图形和交互技术领域研究有卓越成就的个人。

9. **Significant New Researcher Award** 卓越创新研究学者奖：该奖项主要颁发给近期在计算机图形领域作出了重大贡献的新人。

10. **Outstanding Service Award** 杰出服务奖：是在偶数年颁发给为ACM SIGGRAPH服务的优秀志愿者。

11. **Distinguished Artist Award** 杰出艺术家奖：ACM SIGGRAPH设立，主要颁发给创造了杰出艺术作品的艺术家，其作品都是在数字艺术领域极具美学价值的。

12. **Animation Theater and Electronic Theater presentations** 动画剧场和电子剧场展映：是SIGGRAPH展会的重要组成部分和最引人注目的亮点。众多数字艺术家和电脑动画创作者都会将他们最杰出的艺术作品集中在年会上展示，Pixar(皮克斯)、ILM(工业光魔)等著名动画以及电影特效公司都会在大会上发布新近创作的动画短片和电影片段。每年SIGGRAPH都会出版动画剧场和电子剧场DVD专辑。

13. **machine interactivity** 机器互动：指人机交互、人机互动(Human–Computer Interaction或Human–Machine Interaction，简称HCI或HMI)，是一门研究系统与用户之间的互动关系的学问。

14. ***The Adventures of André & Wally B.***《安德列与威利的冒险》：1984年约翰·拉斯特(John Lasseter)加盟乔治·卢卡斯的电脑特效公司后开始创作自己的第一部三维动画短片。这是一部片长度只有2分钟的动画短片，片中人物造型都是由简单的集合体拼接而成。

15. **The SIGGRAPH Asia Conference SIGGRAPH** 亚洲会议：2008 年，SIGGRAPH 根据全球发展趋势，将 SIGGRAPH 年会分成夏季大会和冬季大会。夏季大会仍然按惯例在北美重要城市举办，冬季大会在亚洲重要城市举办。

16. **the Suntec Singapore International Convention and Exhibition Centre** 新达新加坡国际会议与展览中心：位于新加坡的核心地带新达城，是新加坡三大会展中心之一，为国际一流的会展重地。

17. **Pacifico Yokohama** 横滨太平洋会展中心：位于神奈川县横滨市西区，是一座国际级别的集会议、展览和宾馆于一体的复合设施。

18. **COEX Convention & Exhibition Center Seoul** 首尔会议暨展览中心：位于韩国首尔江南商业区的心脏地带的一个商业和文化中心，是韩国重要的会展中心，也是韩国韩国顶级商务活动重要聚集地。

Comprehensive Questions

1. What functions does the ACM SIGGRAPH Digital Arts Community perform?
2. If you were given the chance to give a plenary lecture at SIGGRAPH Asia 2011, what topic would you choose? Why?

Further Reading

◎ ***CG101:A Computer Graphics Industry Reference***

Author: Terrence Masson

Publisher: Digital Fauxtography; 2nd edition (2007)

Web Links

www.siggraph.org

www.animation-festivals.com

16 CHAPTER

Text

Academy of Motion Picture Arts and Sciences

The **Academy of Motion Picture Arts and Sciences**[1] is the world's preeminent movie-related organization, with a membership of more than 6,000 of the most accomplished men and women working in cinema. Although best known for its annual Oscar telecast, the Academy is involved in a wide array of education, outreach, preservation and research activities. The Academy derives the majority of its revenue from the licensing of broadcast rights to the annual Academy Awards presentation. The current president of the Academy is **Tom Sherak**[2].

The Academy operates some non-Awards activities and facilities: **Margaret Herrick Library**[3] is the Academy's renowned library, it has one of the world's most extensive and comprehensive research collections on the subject of motion pictures; Academy Film Archive is dedicated to the preservation and study of motion pictures, the Archive collects, restores, documents and provides research access to films; Science and Technology Council provides a forum for technological cooperation within the entertainment industry, and preserves the history of motion picture science and technology; The Academy presents a busy year-round calendar of film retrospectives,

lecture series and exhibitions; It also provides financial grants to film-related organizations and institutions, educates high school students about the crafts of filmmaking, and encourages and recognizes the achievements of future filmmakers.

Galleries & theaters

The Academy's numerous and diverse operations are housed in three facilities in the Los Angeles area: the headquarters building in Beverly Hills, which was constructed specifically for the Academy, and two Centers for Motion Picture Study – one in Beverly Hills, the other in **Hollywood**[4] – which were existing structures restored and transformed to contain the Academy's Library, Film Archive and other departments and programs. The Academy's main building in Beverly Hills houses two galleries that are open free to the public. The **Grand Lobby Gallery**[5] and the Fourth Floor Gallery offer changing exhibits related to films, film-making and film personalities.

The **Samuel Goldwyn Theater**[6] seats 1,012, and was designed to present films at maximum technical accuracy, with state-of-the-art_projection equipment and sound system. Located in the headquarters building, the theater is busy year-round with the Academy's public programming, members-only screenings, **movie premieres**[7] and other special activities (including the live television broadcast of the Academy Awards nominations announcement every January). The Academy Little Theater is a 67-seat screening facility also located at the Academy's headquarters in Beverly Hills. The **Linwood Dunn Theater**[8] is located at the Academy's **Pickford Center for Motion Picture Study**[9] in Hollywood and seats 286 people. There is also a theater for New York-based Academy events, Academy Theater at Lighthouse International.

Membership

Membership in the Academy is by invitation only. Invitation comes from the Board of Governors. Membership eligibility may be achieved by earning a competitive Oscar nomination or an existing member may submit a name based on other significant contribution to the field of motion pictures.

New membership proposals are considered annually. The Academy does not publicly disclose its full membership, although press releases have announced the names of those who have recently been invited to join.Academy membership is divided into 15 branches, representing different disciplines in motion pictures. Members may not belong to more than one branch. Members whose work does not fall within one of the branches may belong to a group known as "Members At Large." Members at Large have all the privileges of branch membership except for representation on the Board.

Associate members are those closely allied to the industry but not actively engaged in motion picture production. They are not represented on the Board and do not vote on Academy Awards.

Academy Branches

- Actors
- Art Directors
- **Cinematographers**[10]
- Directors
- Documentary
- Executives
- Film Editors
- **Makeup Artists & Hairstylists**[11]
- Music
- Producers
- Public Relations
- Short Films and Feature Animation
- Sound
- Visual Effects
- Writers

Words and Phrases

preeminent [pri'eminənt]
adj. 卓越的；超群的

accomplished [ə'kɔmpliʃt]
adj. 有修养的；有学问的；技术熟练的

telecast ['telikɑ:st]
电视节目转播

be dedicated to
奉献给，献身于；专注于

council ['kaunsəl]
n. 委员会；理事会

forum ['fɔ:rəm]
n. 论坛，讨论会

retrospective [,retrəu'spektiv]
n. 回顾展

lecture series
n. 系列讲座

diverse [dai'və:s]
adj. 不同的；多种多样的

Beverly Hills
比弗利山庄，位于洛杉矶在好莱坞附近

archive ['ɑ:kaiv]
n. 档案馆；资料馆

invitation [,invi'teiʃən]
n. 邀请，请柬

eligibility [,elidʒə'biləti]
n. 被选举资格

significant [sig'nifikənt]
adj. 重大的；有效的；有意义的

proposal [prəu'pəuzəl]
n. 提案；提议

press release
新闻发布；新闻稿

discipline ['disiplin]
n. 学科

fall within
属于…之列，在…范围内

privilege ['privilidʒ]
n. 特权；优待

associate member
n. 准会员

ally to
与…关联

engage in
从事于，参加

vote on
就…表决

Notes

1. **Academy of Motion Picture Arts and Sciences** 美国电影艺术与科学学会：1927 年 5 月 11 日在美国加利福尼亚州洛杉矶建立，是奥斯卡奖的主办单位。它的主要目标是促进电影业内在文化、教育、技术等领域的相互合作，表彰为电影业作出杰出贡献的人士，为各界人士提供公共的论谈与交流的机会，表达电影制作人的观点，并为专业人士与大众提供相关的教育及学习活动。道格拉斯·范朋克(Douglas Fairbanks)是学院的第一任主席，现任主席是汤姆·谢拉克(Tom Sherak)。官方网址：www.oscars.org。

2. **Tom Sherak** 汤姆 · 谢拉克：2009 年当选新一届美国电影艺术与科学学会主席。此前他已在学会的行政部门工作了 6 年，曾担任 20 世纪福克斯公司(20th Century Fox)的高级主管，同时兼任加利福尼亚大学的客座教授，曾参与影片《华尔街》、《异形》等影片。

3. **Margaret Herrick Library** 玛格丽特·赫里克图书馆：美国电影艺术与科学学会所属机构，建于 1928 年，1991 年迁至现今所在地——加州比弗利山庄(Beverly Hills)的拉辛尼伦吉大道(La Cienega Boulevard)。图书馆以第一位管理员并担任长期执行理事的玛格丽特 · 赫里克(Margaret Herrick 1902-1976)的名字命名，致力于电影艺术及工业历史的展示，包括从默片时代起的电影服装设计草图、道具手稿、照片、海报、电影剪辑、乐谱及录音资料等珍贵收藏品。2002 年，为纪念学会的第一任会长、著名的演员和电影制作人道哥拉斯 · 范朋克(Douglas Fairbanks)，机构被命名为范朋克电影研究中心(Fairbanks Center for Motion Picture Study)。

4. **Hollywood** 好莱坞：本意上是一个地名的概念，港译“荷里活”，是全球最著名的影视娱乐和旅游热门地点，位于美国加利福尼亚州洛杉矶市市区西北郊。现“好莱坞”一词用来指代美国加州南部的电影工业。

5. **Grand Lobby Gallery** 位于电影艺术与科学学会总部底层的大厅画廊，有超过 4000 平方英尺的展览空间，可容纳 1000 人。

6. **Samuel Goldwyn Theater** 塞缪尔 · 戈德温剧院：位于洛杉矶比弗利山庄，为纪念美国电影制作人、电影工业的先驱之一塞缪尔 · 戈德温(Samuel Goldwyn 1882—1974)而建。戈德温的作品《黄金时代》获得 1946 年奥斯卡奖。他因制作场面宏大的高质量电影而著称。

7. **movie premiere** 电影首映式

8. **Linwood Dunn Theater** 林伍德·邓恩剧院：奥斯卡评审剧院之一，位于碧克馥电影研究中心大楼内，是学会最新建设的剧院，可容纳 286 人，拥有最先进的放映系统。

9. **Pickford Center for Motion Picture Study** 碧克馥电影研究中心：是电影艺术与科学学会三个洛杉矶分支机构之一，坐落于好莱坞中心地带。中心的命名是为了纪念伟大的默片时代的女演员玛丽·碧克馥 (Mary Pickford)，她是美国电影艺术与科学学院的创始人之一。电影艺术与科学学会的许多部门就在中心所在的大楼里面，包括电影档案馆(Academy Film Archive)、科学与技术委员会(Science and Technology Council)、尼科尔剧本写作奖项目(Nicholl Fellowship)办公室。这座建筑于 1948 年启用，被誉为好莱坞最古老的大楼之一。

10. **cinematographer** 电影摄影师

11. **Makeup Artists & Hairstylists** 化妆师和发型师

Comprehensive Questions

1. “The Academy …educates high school students about the crafts of filmmaking.” ——do you think this is necessary? Why?
2. How is the Academy’s membership eligibility achieved?
3. Do you know why Academy Awards is also called as Oscar?

Further Reading

◎***80 Years of the Oscar: The Official History of the Academy Awards***

Author：Robert Osborne

Publisher：Abbeville Press (2008)

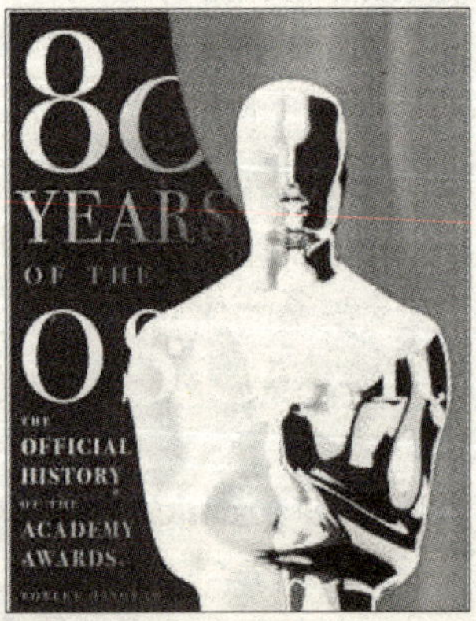

◎***Chris Gore's Ultimate Film Festival Survival Guide: The Essential Companion for Filmmakers and Festival-Goers***

Author：Chris Gore

Publisher：Lone Eagle; 4th edition (2009)

Web Links

www.oscars.org

17 CHAPTER

Text

California Institute of the Arts[1]

"What young artists need is a school where they can learn a variety of skills, a place where there is cross-pollination. The remarkable thing that's taking place in almost every field of endeavor is an accelerating rate of dynamic growth and change. The arts, which have historically symbolized the advance of human progress, must match this growth if they are going to maintain their value in and influence on society. The talents of musicians, the self expression of the actor, and the techniques and applications of fine and commercial artist are being used more and more in today's buiness-not by themselves but rather, in close association with each other. What we must have, then, is a completely new approach to training in the arts-an entirely new educational concept which will properly prepare artists and give them the vital tools so necessary for working in, and drawing from, every field of creativity and performance. There is an urgent need for a professional school which will not only give its students thorough training in a specific field, but will also allow the widest possible range of artistic growth and expression. To meet this need is exactly why California Institute of the Arts has been created, and why we all believe so strongly in its importance. Students will be able to take anything - art, drama, music, dance, writing. They'll graduate with a degree of Bachelor of Fine Arts. The student body of CalArts shouldn't be over two thousand, and as many as possible should reside on campus. There should be some allowance for those who are talented, they should be able to express themselves without worrying about grades. There will be a lot of scholarships at CalArts. Those who can pay will pay; those who can't will get scholarships. We don't want any dilettantes at CalArts. We want people with talent. That will be the one factor in getting into CalArts: talent. If I can help provide a place to develop the talent of the future, I think I will have accomplished something."

—Disney himself has stated of his memorial school

The California Institute of the Arts, commonly referred to as CalArts, is located in Valencia, in Los Angeles County, California. Incorporated in 1961 as the first degree-granting institution of higher learning in the United States created specifically for students of both the visual and the performing arts.

This school created by **Walt Disney**[2] and staffed by an alternative array of professionals, the institute was started as Disney's dream of an interdisciplinary "Caltech of the arts." CalArts provides a collaborative environment for all sorts of artists. Students are free to develop their own work in a workshop atmosphere, as respected members of a community of artists in which authority is constantly tested and where teaching works through persuasion rather than coercion. Intercultural exchange among artists helps in practicing and understanding of the art making process in the broadest context possible.

Schools and degree programs available at CalArts include: School of Art; School of Critical Studies;The Sharon Lund School of Dance; School of Film/Video; The Herb Alpert School of Music and School of Theater.

The **School of Film/Video**[3] is one of the nation's premiere colleges for studying the art of the moving image. It is singularly devoted to filmmaking as a personal, independent art form. The School is especially unique in that it promotes the studies of all major types of filmmaking: dramatic narrative, documentary, experimental live-action, **character-based animation**[4], **experimental animation**[5], multimedia, and **installation**[6]. We offer four challenging programs, each one with its own specialized curriculum focusing on specific areas in filmmaking. At the same time, all four share an ethos in **combining rigorous practical training with theoretical inquiry, hands-on production with aesthetic reflection**[7]. The Notable alumnis include **Tim Burton**[8] (79, Character Animation), **John Lasseter**[9] (BFA 79, Character Animation) ,Henry Selick (MFA 77, Experimental Animation) ,etc.

Words and Phrases

cross-pollination ['krɔ:s,pɔli'neiʃən]
n. 知识、思想等的分享、交流

endeavor [in'devə]
n. 努力；尽力

dynamic [dai'næmik]
adj. 动态的；动力的；动力学的；有活力的

symbolize ['simbəlaiz]
v. 象征

talent ['tælənt]
n. 才能；天才；天资

application [,æpli'keiʃən]
n. 适用性；实用性

vital ['vaitəl]
adj. 至关重要的

urgent ['ə:dʒənt]
adj. 紧急的；急迫的

reside [ri'zaid]
vt. 住，居住；属于

allowance [ə'lauəns]
n. 津贴

dilettante [,dili'tænti, 'dilitɑ:nt]
n. 业余爱好者；一知半解者

Incorporate [in'kɔ:pəreit, in'kɔ:pərət]
vi. 合并；组成

interdisciplinary [,intə'disiplinəri]
跨领域学科；交叉学科

Caltech (California Institute of Technology)
加利福尼亚州理工学院，是美国的一所久负盛名的大学

authority [ɔ:'θɔrəti]
n. 权威；权力

test [test]
v. 考查；考验

coercion [kəu'ə:ʃən]
n. 强制；强迫

devoted to
专心于…

curriculum [kə'rikjuləm]
n. 课程

ethos ['iːθɔs]
个人(或集团)的特性、性格、气质、信仰等

rigorous ['rigərəs]
adj. 严格的，严厉的

inquiry [in'kwaiəri]
n. 探究；调查

alumni [ə'lʌmnai]
n. 校友；男毕业生

Notes

1. **California Institute of the Arts** 加州艺术学院：是国际上最具影响的艺术学院之一，1961年由华特 · 迪士尼创建，是美国唯一的一所集音乐、舞蹈、美术、电影、戏剧、写作于一体的综合艺术学院。成立以来，培养出无数杰出的艺术创作者，如：现任皮克斯首席创意官的约翰 · 拉斯特(John Lasseter)，《鬼妈妈》的导演亨利 · 塞利克(Henry Selick)与电影奇才蒂姆·伯顿(Tim Burton)等。官方网址：www.calarts.edu。

2. **Walt Disney** 华特 · 迪士尼：1901 年生于芝加哥，创造了当今最具规模的卡通及娱乐媒体王国。他凭借在电影叙事与制作上的才能，带领着优秀的团队制作出一部部精彩的动画作品。代表作有《白雪公主》(*Snow White*)、《幻想曲》(*Fantasia*)、《灰姑娘》(*Cinderella*)、《小飞侠》 (*Peter Pan*)等。

3. **School of Film/Video** 加州艺术学院的影视学院，有电影制作、实验动画、角色动画、电影编导等专业。

4. **character-based animation** 角色动画

5. **experimental animation** 实验动画：指非商业的探索性质的动画作品，其特点是运用多种材料进行视觉影像的实验。实验动画最早诞生在法国，在各国开始流行，对世界动画的发展产生了深刻的影响。

6. **installation** 装置艺术：艺术家在特定的时空环境里，将人类日常生活中的已消费或未消费过的物质文化实体，进行艺术性地选择、改造、组合，以令其演绎出新的表达个体或群体精神文化意蕴的艺术形态。

7. **combining rigorous practical training with theoretical inquiry, hands-on production with aesthetic reflection** 加州艺术学院所倡导的教学思想，即“严谨的实际训练和理论研究相结合；动手能力和美学修养相结合”。

8. **Tim Burton** 蒂姆·伯顿：美国电影导演，1958 年生于加州的伯班克(Burbank)。毕业于加州艺术学院，之后成为迪士尼动画师。蒂姆·伯顿的影片善于运用象征和隐喻的手法，视角独特。其代表作有《蝙蝠侠》(*Batman*)、《大鱼》(*Big Fish*)、《剪刀手爱德华》(*Edward Scissorhands*)等。与亨利·塞利克(Henry Selick)合作过《圣诞夜惊魂》(*The Nightmare Before Christmas*)等多部动画电影。

9. **John Lasseter** 约翰·拉斯特：迪士尼和皮克斯动画工作室的首席创意官，1957 年生于美国加州，加州艺术学院毕业之后进入了迪士尼公司。20 世纪 90 年代创立皮克斯公司，导演了《玩具总动员》(*Toy Story*)、《虫虫危机》(*A Bug's Life*)、《赛车总动员》(*Cars*)等作品。

Comprehensive Questions

1. Try to explain the collaborative atmosphere of CalArts.
2. What is unique about the School of Film/Video?
3. “Combining rigorous practical training with theoretical inquiry, hands-on production with aesthetic reflection”——how do you appreciate the common ethos of the School’s programs?

Further Reading

◎ ***Creative Colleges: A Guide for Student Actors, Artists, Dancers, Musicians and Writers***

Author: Elaina Loveland

Publisher: Supercollege, Llc (2010)

◎ ***What They Don't Teach You at Film School: 161 Strategies For Making Your Own Movie No Matter What***

Author: Camille Landau & Tiare White

Publisher: Hyperion (2000)

Web Links

www.calarts.edu

www.filmschools.com

18 CHAPTER

Text

Japan Animation Industry Trends

Summary

Japanese animation is in the spotlight not only in Japan, but overseas as well. Amid an expanding of domestic market for films, television and videos, Japanese animation film producers have also turned their eyes toward overseas markets. At the same time, new developments have been seen in terms of diversified funding methods for film production. Against this background, the Japanese animation industry is working hard to overcome shortages such as human-resource skills, reductions in domestic film-production sites and the challenge of expanding operations overseas.

Market Overview

The talk of the Japan animation market in 2004 was Studio Ghibli's smash hit, *Howl'sMoving Castle*, which opened in November and was the studio's first new release in three years. Director Hayao Miyazaki's work exceeded 10 million viewers in just 44 days, faster than any other movie in Japan. Its popularity continued thereafter, with viewers rising to 14.23 million on March 8, 2005, which broke records of the mark set by Miyazaki's *Princess Mononoke* and ranked as number two in Japanese film history. Miyazaki's *Spirited Away* won the feature length animation Oscar at the 75th Academy Awards in 2003, reprising its capture of the **Golden Bear**[1] at the 2002 Berlin Film Festival and proving once again Japan was able to produce world-level animation. Director **Mamoru Oshii**'s[2] animated film ***Innocence***[3] was nominated for an award at the 57th Cannes film festival in 2004. *Innocence* is the sequel to ***Ghost in the Shell***[4] (1995), which reached number one on ***Billboard***'s[5] video chart in the United States.

Nonetheless, the industry has not yet shifted its posture sufficiently to respond to overseas acclaim. Moving forward, the Japanese anime industry must not only expand overseas, but develop the necessary production/distribution systems and personnel to capitalize on the global business opportunities. Production systems have in fact been set up, but the industry still has many glaring weaknesses in domestic/overseas distribution and rights, such as licensing and international business expertise in general. In the field of personnel development, animators do not have a suitably high social standing, so the exodus of such personnel to other industries and countries has become a large problem.

Shifting Market Size

Japan's domestic anime market can be broadly divided into three categories:

1) Feature-length films

2) TV shows

3) Video and DVD versions of the above two, and original productions

According to the **Media Development Research Institute**[6], Japan's anime market sales fell 10.4% to 191.2 billion yen in 2003, including box office revenues for anime films, TV animation production fees and profits from sales and rental of video and DVD titles. This was the first decline in two years (Fig. 1). The substantial gains realized in 2001 and 2002 were mainly attributed to *Spirited Away*'s success at the box office (30.4 billion yen) in 2001 and then in DVD form in 2002. The lack of this sort of hit led to market contraction in 2003, but sales are estimated to have grown in 2004 thanks to the success of *Howl's Moving Castle*.

The market for anime content, including character licensing/merchandising, selling rights to use character images on other products and the sale of character toys, is estimated to be worth about two trillion yen.

Fig. 1 Anime Market Size (Film, TV and Video)

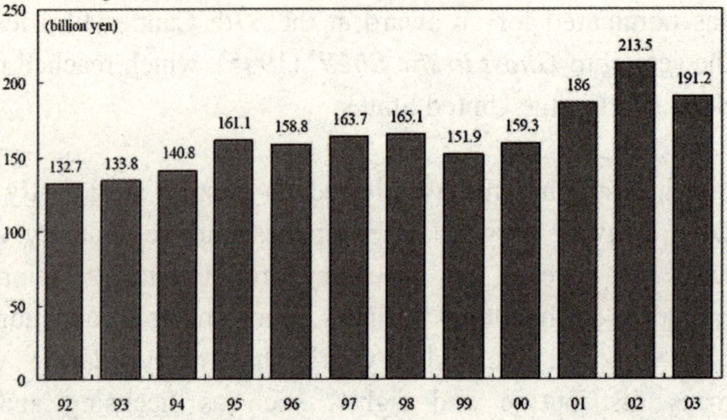

Source: Dentsu Communication Institute Inc.

Words and Phrases

in the spotlight
处于公众注意的中心

amid [ə'mid]
prep. 在…之中；在…过程中，在…期间

domestic market
国内市场

overseas market
海外市场

diversified [dai'və:sifaid]
adj. 多样化的；各种的

human-resource
人力资源

smash hit
巨大的成功；轰动一时的人物

reprise [ri'pri:z, ri'praiz]
vt. 重复；再一次

sequel ['si:kwel, -wəl]
n. 续集；结局

nonetheless [,nʌnðə'les]
conj. 尽管如此，但是

sufficiently [sə'fiʃəntli]
adv. 充分地；足够地

capitalize on
利用

in fact
事实上，实际上

glaring [glɛəriŋ]
adj. 耀眼的

license ['laisəns]
v. 许可；批准

expertise [,ekspə:'ti:z]
n. 专门知识；专门技术

social standing
社会地位

exodus ['eksədəs]
n. 大批的离去，(移民)出国

revenue ['revənju:]
n. 收入，收益

profit ['prɔfit]
n. 利润；利益

decline [di'klain]
n. 下降；衰退

substantial gains
实质性的收益

lead to
导致；通向

contraction [kən'trækʃən]
n. 收缩

estimate ['estimeit]
vi. 估计；判断

merchandising ['mə:tʃəndaiziŋ]
n. 推销；销售规划

Notes

1. **Golden Bear** 金熊奖：是柏林国际电影节(BerlinInternational Film Festival)授予电影作品的最高奖项，设置最佳故事片、纪录片、科教片、美术片等。
2. **Mamoru Oshii** 押井守：日本著名动画电影导演，1951 年生于日本东京，东京学艺大学教育学系美术组毕业。代表作有《福星小子》、《机动警察》、《攻壳机动队》等。
3. ***Ghost in the Shell 2:Innocence***《攻壳机动队 2》：押井守导演动画作品，2004 年在日本上映，获得日本 SF 大奖。
4. ***Ghost in the Shell***《攻壳机动队》：押井守作品，1995 年在日本上映。
5. ***Billboard***《公告牌》杂志：1894 年创刊于美国俄亥俄州辛辛那提市，初期内容以州内大事、狂欢节日、娱乐演出为主。1954 年后，《公告牌》杂志掌控了整个美国流行乐界，包括各类流行榜单的排行信息，先后推出单曲销量榜、Hot 100 单曲榜、Pop 100 单曲榜等权威榜单。
6. **Media Development Research Institute** 日本媒体发展研究所

Comprehensive Questions

1. What are the weaknesses of Japan's animation industry?
2. What caused Japan's anime market sales fall in 2003?

Further Reading

◎ ***Animation: Art and Industry***

Editor: Maureen Furniss

Publisher: John Libbey Publishing (2009)

◎ ***The Anime Encyclopedia: A Guide to Japanese Animation Since 1917***

Author: Jonathan Clementslen, Helen McCarthy

Publisher: Stone Bridge Press; Revised and Expanded edition (2006)

Web Links

www.aidb.com

www.animationnation.com

附录Ⅰ：Translation of Texts 参考译文

Part 1 基础篇

Chapter 1 Animation History 动画简史

动画是展示多个画面连续运动的系列图像，这些单个画面是由摄影机拍摄而成，并且是互相关联的。每个画面之间都会有细微的改变，因为这样可以使它们在连续播放的时候（每秒 24 帧）呈现流畅的画面。

动画的早期开创者包括美国的温瑟·麦凯、法国的埃米尔·科尔和乔治·梅里爱。大多数人认同 1918 年由温瑟·麦凯制作的《露斯坦尼亚号之沉没》(Sinking of the Lusitania) 是第一部真正意义上的动画片。

在 1910 年以前的早期动画片，每次只能进行简单的图片拍摄。动画制作的劳动强度非常大，每分钟的电影都要绘制成百张的图像。直到 1913 年赛璐珞被应用到动画制作上，使得动画的制作效率得以提高。透明赛璐珞胶片的利用，代替了繁多的画稿绘制过程。动画师可以制作更加复杂的背景和前景效果，中间是活动的角色层。这样动画家可以不用在每一张动画纸上重复描画背景，只需将活动形象与不动的背景分层，让角色移动其中。同时它也出现了一种特殊的视觉效果，当前景物体移动的时候和背景之间形成一种有深度的空间感。

是华特·迪士尼将动画影片提升到了一个新的境界。1928 年在《蒸汽机船威利》首映之时，迪士尼第一次把自己的卡通影片加入了声音效果。1937 年他又创作了世界上第一部标准长度的动画电影《白雪公主》。

伴随计算机动画技术的介入，动画创作被赋予了全新的内涵。许多电影加入了由计算机制作的动画特效。由卢卡斯导演的《星球大战》系列，在制作上很大程度上依赖于计算机动画技术。1995 年由迪士尼影片公司和皮克斯动画工作室合作推出的三维动画片《玩具总动员》，成为首部完全运用计算机技术制作的动画电影长片。

随着个人计算机的普及，使普通大众成为动画师的梦想有可能变成现实。

Chapter 2　Beginners (1) 动画基础(1)

“animate”一词来源于拉丁语动词“animare”，有“赋予生命”的意思。我们最天真烂漫的梦想和古怪的想法都可以在动画世界中得以实现。动画常常运用绘画、黏土、人偶等各种媒介制作作品，将之呈现在电脑屏幕上，它们看起来如此真实，以至于我们不得不相信那些角色是有生命的。

动画是以视觉方式呈现给观众的，当你写作时，设法使鲜活的电影画面在你的头脑里行进。将文字进行视觉化转换是十分必要的事情。许多卡通剧本作家同时也是画家，他们通过绘画或草图来勾勒他们的想法。好的动画作品是需要故事情节的，而不应像拍电视一样仅仅看到一些头部特写。尽管汉纳·巴贝拉公司的作品以低成本动画闻名，但约瑟夫·巴贝拉曾经告诉自己的分镜头画师：如果仅用六幅画面就能表现人物说话的场景，那么员工们一定会得到惩罚。一定要用视觉来讲故事，动画必须是活灵活现的！

时间和空间是动画创作中的基本要素。观众接收动画信息的速度非常快，哪怕是简短的几个瞬间，观众都会在观看过程中迅速地捕捉到各种信息。时间要素在动画中是非常重要的，正像在滑稽剧表演中，画面的速度是极快的，所以通常情况下，比起实景影片的拍摄，动画影片脚本会有更多的分镜画面，这都由动画片快速移动的性质所决定的。

动画师在描绘运动时经常运用强化的夸张手法，喜剧演出也常喜欢追求极限。在真人实景拍摄中看上去不可能的有趣情节运用在动画片中往往会引起更加生动的效果。但随着特效技术的日益发展，没有多少场景是在动画中能实现而在实景拍摄中实现不了的。

剧本

动画通常由脚本创作开始——如果没有脚本，至少应有一份书面形式的情节大纲来表达想法。在电视创作中，每个情节段落通常需要一页纸的准备提纲，当计划批准之后，它就会被扩展成情节大纲，最后再将大纲扩展成为一个完整的剧本。一些电影长片和电视卡通短片可能没有具体的剧本，创意主要在分镜头脚本过程中完成。每一部电视系列节目都有一个剧本编审，由他负责整个进程的管理。

制片人和导演对完成的剧本有审批权。制片人和导演这两个职位在美国没有精确和标准的定义，在不同的工作室分工略有不同，有时可以互换担任彼此的工作。独立制片人还要处理更多的资金和预算问题，在一些大型的动画工作室中制作人可以更直接地参与制作过程。

录音

脚本定稿时，接下来的任务便是选定演员进行录音。通常采取演员接到文字稿本进行单独录音的方式，如果准备及时，演员们也会花时间来熟悉人物设计或分镜头脚本，此时由声音导演进行指导。有些工作室倾向于同时为电视动画节目进行一次性录音的方式，正如他们在录制广播剧中所做的。然而，配音演员有时可能会要求分开录制某段对白，尤其是在制作动画长片项目之时。独立的录音方式会更容易地安排演员的时间，这样的分工使制作程序顺利行进以便在编辑影片时精准的调整对白时间。作曲家通常从影片的早期阶段即开始配乐的创作。

分镜头脚本

故事板艺术家通过对剧本的推敲创作出故事的可视化形象，虽然刚开始的描绘有些粗略，但对话和情节已经和每组画面一一匹配。通常，分镜头脚本制作完成后将被扫描拍摄成动态故事板视频样片，动态故事板中已包括影片需要的各种音效，这种方式可以让导演从整体上把握影片的结构并且有效地控制时间长度。

对于动画长片来说，需要大概一年的时间来进行分镜头脚本的创作。在视觉化的开发过程中，剧本或大纲也将进行相应的调整。经过清理的长篇故事板稿本制作成翻页动画书进行审阅，最后，稿本被扫描或拍摄后，将录制好的声音加入其中，制作成为故事录影带。在制作动态故事板或故事录影带过程中，可根据需要对发现的问题进行及时修改。故事录影带的制作贯穿整个动画片生产过程，之后是关键帧的绘制，直到最后动画的完成。

Chapter 3　Beginners (2) 动画基础(2)

背景设计

在动画制作中，美工师或背景画师负责影片背景画面的设计任务，通常情况是一个背景画师先绘制出主要背景画面，其他背景绘制任务则在其他国家通过代工方式完成，这些额外的背景绘制工作细节要和之前的工作严格匹配。由于高昂的成本，只有很少的动画产品在美国本土制作完成。在长篇动画的生产过程中，视觉艺术家往往要同时关注故事情节与画面设计两项任务，在最后的设计方案选定前，要绘制很多概念草图。背景艺术家经常采用传统作画方式，但如今很多动画元素可以通过电脑绘制完成。

色彩设计

色彩造型师在艺术指导的监督下，为场景选择和设计色彩的应用种类。色彩造型的重要性在于，所使用的色彩不仅整体感觉相互协调，而且也能使处于背景中的人物突出、鲜明。

布局设计

布局设计是对于所有故事分镜头的详细描述和展示，是一些画面之间的情节的细分。它们包括每个画面的前景、后景和人物动作开始到停止之间的画面特效。构图师将会进一步对每个拍摄镜头进行提炼，设置摄影机角度，安排摄影机运动方式，加之构图、演出布局、灯光等的处理。画面要按正确的比例设置尺寸和模型。关键的构图画面可能在产品制作运往国外之前就做好了，除此之外的画稿将由国外的动画家完成。如果我们在分镜头的时候就开始制作详细的故事图，布局设计这一阶段也基本上可能被跳过。在这之后，这些画面被放大成正确的尺寸，拆分的画面将作为设计稿来运用在创作中。

动画阶段

动画师接下来要检查之前的配音段落是否完整，然后要落实分镜头脚本以及角色设计的修改完成情况，确定最终的设计稿；动画师还要一层层详细填写摄影表中的各种安排方案。拍摄用画稿不仅要求按照摄制标准格式进行整理，同时也要求让设计稿画师和背景画师对之一一过目，可以采取打孔穿连的方式将画稿按正确顺序一一排列。对于动画长片来说，之前的线拍测试会有效地检阅动画过程的正确性。对于电视和录影带版的制作而言，关键帧画师要绘制出动画中最重要的动作细节，以便作品送往海外的加工能顺利进行。

清稿画师或助理动画师对之前通过铅笔稿审查的动画进行清理，然后根据需要对关键动作进一步补充，配合中间画动画师的工作，以完整地呈现动画中间的各种动作。最后由视觉特效师来完成诸如火焰、水纹等特殊效果。对于传统长篇动画的制作，作品是由一张张静止画面连续拍摄而成，每一分钟影片就需要大概 1400 张手绘画稿，所以，动画制作的劳动强度可想而知。

场面调度

场景规划师负责对每个场景所包含的视觉元素进行分解，考查如何对视觉元素进行舍去和移动。此项工作现在可以方便地在电脑中完成，这能确保他们能以有效的方式完成任务。这些专家掌握扎实的技术知识，他们要检查所有数据，让场景中的摄影机找到最佳的移动设置方式。他们还为画师对色彩效果的选择提供参考。

Chapter 4 Basic Animation Writing Structure 动画剧作的基本结构

重视结构有助于写出一个好的故事剧本。然而，故事长度的不同，其结构的复杂程度也不同；不同的类型（专题节目、少儿卡通、网络短剧）或不同的题材（动作类、冒险类、喜剧类、儿童类），也会影响到结构的复杂程度和故事的整体风格。专题类脚本比较长，需要较复杂的结构才能引起我们的兴趣；网络短剧或一分钟电视卡通则不需要太多的情节。事实上，结构可能会影响到剧中的笑料。一般而言，比起依靠笑料来推动情节的喜剧片，动作片或冒险片需要更复杂的情节来呈现；黄金时段的动画片往往使用情景喜剧的结构样式，这种样式以机智幽默的对白为主，同时辅以较少的人物动作。

基本结构

所有的故事都应有开端、中段和结局。一部系列短剧（适合在电视或网络上播放）必须有主角并且以他们为中心展开剧情；简单说来每段情节的主演或者主要人物一定要有一个目标或者动机，要设置一些人或一些事去反对这一目标。这些是基本的故事要素，也同样适用于一部电影。当然，也有比较抽象且不以讲故事为目标的独立动画电影。

剧本常用的三幕结构：

第一幕　问题已经确立。(一个女孩在旗杆顶)

第二幕　在高潮之前。(有人向她扔西红柿和烂橘子)

第三幕　结局,以画龙点睛的结尾使事件告一段落。(她寻找到从旗杆顶部下来的方法)

有时，一部电视动画剧本只能写成两幕，也只能是两幕，在两幕长度的基础上当然也可以扩展成三幕的结构样式。标准三幕式结构的电视剧本长度大致是一样的，只是最后的一幕可能是最短的，又或者是第一幕比较短。电视剧集通常被插播的商业广告中断，因此，为了让观众坐在位子上看完广告，就必须增强故事的悬念，一部公开播放的可引起人好奇的预告片就可达到这一目标。

一个三幕结构的剧本按比例可分配如下:第一幕占 25%,第二幕占 50%,第三幕占 25%。这个比例不是一成不变的。

故事的主题

主题是指主角得到的经验教训，故事的主要启示或价值观。当我们谈论主角本身时，我们只是简略触摸到故事的主题。并非是所有的动画都有故事主题，但是许多好故事肯定都有。对观众而言，主题是稍后才会考虑到的，它会给故事一些补充，有助于我们理解彼此以及身边的世界。它是基于我们的生活和世俗人类所作出的一些评论，有助于我们与剧中人物产生共鸣。我们从中看到自己的问题，并鼓励剧中人去解决那些问题，去克服自身缺点，以便满足生存和成长的需要。

通常一个主题被看做是一种价值与另一种价值的冲突，并最后获胜，如宽恕战胜了复仇，活在当下比总是担忧未来会让生活更充实，与你的哥哥在一起嬉闹比独自玩耍更有趣——至少这种乐趣可持续到你被抓住。这些是基本的日常生活价值观，它们在很早的时代就已经成为故事的主题。古老的口头传说；神话；传奇；古希腊、罗马和莎士比亚戏剧；小说；电影；甚至比赛都以这些价值冲突为中心。

牢记你的观众，因为男孩是最大的购票群体，许多以表现孩子童心为中心的电影正在被成人类电影所取代。如果你的观众主要是儿童，那么你要考虑什么样的主题是适当的。对电影来说，在全世界通行的、时刻能触动我们所有人的主题通常就是最好的。

人物，情节和主题都是相关联的。你的男主角有性格方面的缺陷，这个缺陷正在妨碍着他追求幸福。在故事进程中，他所经历的事情不仅改变了他看待生活的方式，同时也将改变他以后的生活。这描摹出主角性格发展的弧度。理想意义上，他将变成一个较完美的人，或起码开始较好地去了解他自身和这个世界。对于你的男主角和其他人来说，达到的目标让生活更美好了吗？男主角的价值观和反派角色的价值观最后谁胜出了，原因是什么？可能不止只有一个主题，但假如这种情况真的存在，那么主题之间必须是相关联的。

主题是具体可感的，不是教条的或说教的，没有人愿意听布道。反而我们想要通过人物的行动表现出他们在生活中的价值，以及他们如何为世界上的美好而奋斗。价值观主要通过行动得以表达，但是，或许也偶尔会在言语冲突的过程中得以显现。冲突和对立的价值观，是所有故事的核心。

Chapter 5 Twelve Basic Principles of Animation (1) 动画的 12 条黄金法则(1)

“动画的 12 条黄金法则”是由迪士尼动画师欧利 · 约翰斯顿（Ollie Johnston）和弗兰克 · 托马斯（Frank Thomas）在他们 1981 年的著作《迪士尼——生命的景象》一书中介绍的制作动画的基本原则。他们的写作基于 20 世纪 30 年代引领迪士尼动画黄金时代的动画师的经典作品，和他们在现实主义动画创作方面的伟大成就。这 12 法则的主要目的是使动画师所塑造的角色形象能够遵循正常的物理原则，除此之外他们也把视角放在类似于人物的情绪刻画和角色的生动性等抽象问题上。

如今这本书所提及的 12 条法则已被动画界广泛采纳，甚至被看做是“行业圣经”。1999 年这本书在“最受欢迎的动画书籍”网络评选中，成为排名第一位的图书。尽管它的初衷是为了给传统手绘动画工作者提供指导，但 12 法则仍然适用于今天广泛流行的电脑动画制作领域。

压缩与伸展

“压缩与伸展”是首先要关注的重要原则，其目的是为了给所绘制的物体充满量感和使其具有弹性。不管是弹跳小圆球这样简单的物体，还是如人物脸部肌肉组织这样复杂的构造，都会运用到此项原理。物体被扔到最高点时，压缩与伸展的数值会达到一个夸张的程度，从而使其运动充满趣味。然而在现实主义动画中，这些法则最重要的方面则体现在：当物体被压缩与伸展时体积不会发生变化。如果球体的长度被垂直拉伸，它的宽度（指在三维世界中）需要进行相应的伸缩。

预备动作

预备动作常应用于一个动作发生之前，强调动作的准备状态，目的是让这个动作看起来更加真实。一个舞者跳离地板前首先需要弯曲双膝；一个打高尔夫球的人打侧飞球时需要先把棍棒向后转。这个技巧同样适用于微小的身体运动，如角色视线离开屏幕预备看某人的到来，或者注意力集中在一个做拾起动作的人身上。在一些特殊情况下，某种被期待的动作的预备状态也可以被省略。突降法的最终效果是使观者产生突然被袭击的感觉，能够增强一场戏的喜剧效果，这种情况经常被称为“突如其来的笑料”。

演出布局

这条法则类似于众所周知的戏剧和电影中的演出布局。它的目的是引导观众的注意力，使其明确一个场景中最重要的要素是什么，正在发生什么和即将发生什么。约翰斯顿和托马斯定义它为“任何想法彻底和准确的体现”，不论那些想法是一个动作，一个人物，一个表情或者是一种情绪，都要充分表述出来。这一原则通过几种方式体现，诸如角色在画面中的位置，灯光和阴影的运用，摄像机的角度和位置等。这条法则的实质是把精力集中在有重要意义的事物上面，避免不必要的细节。

连续运动与姿态对应

这是两种不同的达到写实性绘画的方法。“连续动作”是从第一张开始，依照顺序画到最后一张，而“姿态对应”需要开始时画少量的关键帧，接着补上中间的动画。“连续动作”创建一种更流畅、充满运动感的图像，以更好的表达现实的运动状态。然而另一方面，它却难于全程保持正确的比例和令人信服的姿态。“姿态对应”的优势就在于它能很好地表现戏剧性和感人至深的场景。在实际制作中，这两种方法经常被综合运用。

计算机动画消除了“连续运动”绘制中产生的比例问题；而“姿态对应”因在合成方面的优势，仍然使用计算机动画手段进行处理。计算机的应用促进了传统方法的快速实现，它能够自动弥补动作之间丢失的序列帧画面。然而，在新技术应用的同时遵循这些基本原则仍然是十分必要的。

Chapter 6 Twelve Basic Principles of Animation (2) 动画的12条黄金法则(2)

跟随与重叠动作

“跟随”意味着物体的各个部位在主体角色的动作停止后，仍然保持一定程度的跟随运动。“重叠动作”是指身体在运动中以不同频率姿势的持续状态，产生分离重叠的时间差与夸张的变形。一定要注意的是，这些技巧的运用能增加动画的趣味性与表现力，但现实主义动画必须为动作测定准确的时间，产生令人信服的结果。

慢进与慢出

人类身体的运动和其他多数物体一样，以时间节奏的加速和减慢为前提。正因如此，如果在动画的开始和结束处加入更多的画格而减少中间的帧数，动画看起来就会更加真实。这个法则适用于角色在两个极点姿势间的运动，如坐下和站起；它同样适用于移动的无生命物体，如上面提到过的弹跳球。

弧形运动

人和动物的身体动作大多数时候都是以抛物线的轨迹运行，动画应该更真实地再现这些运动。它可应用于肢体的旋转运动，或沿着抛物线轨迹运动的物体。只有机械运动是个例外，那是典型的直线运动。

第二动作

加入细微的第二动作是为了使主体运动更加真实生动，同时能辅助和促进主体动作的运行。人在行走时能同时摆动他的手臂或放在口袋里，能够说话或者吹口哨，还能够通过面部表情传达他的情感。第二动作的要点是它是为了强化而不是使人对主要动作注意力的转移。如果后者情况发生，最好在刻画中忽视这些动作。

时间节奏和量感

时间节奏在动画中涉及两个概念：物理时间和戏剧性时间。物理上的时间概念是最基本的，就像故事情节是动画叙事的基础一样。在纯物理学层面上，正确的时间节奏能够使物体运动呈现出更加自然的状态，例如推动一个物体，物体的重量决定着所产生动力的大小。而戏剧性时间概念不已自然为依据，多数从经验中把握，它经常能呈现出喜剧性的节奏状态，或传递出深沉的情感。动作的节奏也会影响到角色的个性表达。

夸张

夸张是动画中一种极为有效的塑造形象的手法，在卡通中完全照搬现实会使角色角色显得毫无生气，情节枯燥无味。夸张的程度依据个人对现实的观察或对风格的要求，如漫画手法或艺术化的处理方式。此外其他的夸张手法如超自然或超现实手法的运用，可以是角色的物理特性发生变化或故事情节自身的变化。应用夸张手法时，把握一定程度至关重要，如果一个场景中包含几个要素，应该权衡这些要素之间的夸张关系，避免使观众困惑或大吃一惊。

扎实的绘画

扎实绘画的原则，实际上意味着动画师也要像学院派艺术家一样拥有良好的绘画基础。动画师同样须要有娴熟的绘画技巧，同时掌握基本的解剖学、构图、量感、均衡、光线和阴影等专业常识。那些创造经典的动画师，善于从生活中汲取营养和创作的灵感。值得一提的是约翰斯顿和托马斯警告年轻的动画师不要“照抄”生活。当今的电脑动画师理论上似乎不需要绘画能力，但实际上他们的工作依旧能从理解这些基本的原则中受益。

吸引力

有吸引力的角色并不一定总是值得同情的那个，反派角色和怪物同样具有吸引力——重要的是观众能感受到角色是真实和充满趣味的，有很多诀窍可以拉近角色与观众间的距，如有时候运用一张精致的孩子般的面孔也是个极好的办法。

Part 2 人物篇

Chapter 7 *Ponyo*, or Hayao Miyazaki's Inner Child 宫崎骏访谈录——内心的自我

宫崎骏——当代的电影魔术师、具有诗人气质的导演，兼具奇思妙想和梦幻般画面创造者，今天跟我们一同分享这部最新上映的感人至深的童话寓言——《悬崖上的金鱼公主》。

《哈尔的移动城堡》上映四年之后，这位日本大师推出了他的最新作品，这部影片依然选择运用传统手绘方式，没有电脑的介入。平面化的视觉风格让影片的角色和场景倍感亲切，这些都归功于传统动画所带来的力量。这部影片的灵感来自于海浪席卷之时作者对大海的凝望与思索，他对海浪的细致描写给予特别的关注，影片的创意超越了我们的期待——最重要的是，他挥笔写就了童年岁月的华丽诗篇。

采访

AV：请您先来描述一下这部电影？

HM：这是关于小主人公波妞的故事，一只小人鱼梦想着能和宗介在一起，一个五岁的小男孩承诺一定要要保护好她，也就是讲述小宗介是如何能够遵守他的诺言的。《悬崖上的金鱼公主》是发生在两个孩子之间的友情故事，同时也是一次奇妙的冒险之旅——堪称一部日本版的安徒生童话故事。

海边的一座小城镇、悬崖上的小房子、主人公和大海，所有这一切呈现出栩栩如生的场景，这里每天的生活都充满了惊奇与魔力。故事发展，就如同大海一样，在我们的潜意识世界里，表面是平静的，深处却充满波澜与动荡。随着时空的变换，大海不仅仅成为故事的背景，同时成了最主要的角色。一对小男孩和小女孩、爱与责任、大海与生命，影片所要传达的本质即是：通过这个童话揭示了应对生命中的不幸与不确定性的答案。

AV：在故事的初稿中，您看起来更倾向描写母亲和儿子之间的关系。

HM：当我工作的时候，我时常写下我的想法然后又经常改变很多开始的设计，最初的想法和最终敲定的方案总是不太一样。我最初的想法是描写一个母亲开始，从她生命中寻找自我，包括她和孩子之间的关系。我勾勒出的宗介的妈妈应该是 25 岁左右，但是我的合作者们认为她太年轻了，甚至比他们还小。他们感到画一个 35 岁以下的妈妈是很困难的——没想到我的团队已经变老了……

AV：最后，您的电影的主题是童年，通过那个特别的孩子宗介的眼睛透露出来。

HM：我想让宗介和波妞按照他们自己的意愿自然地生活，影片中有很多那样的场景。当波妞溅宗介水的时候，宗介并不害怕，如果他害怕，他们就不会成为朋友。虽然其他孩子们不喜欢波妞，而只有宗介却从不受此干扰。你看电影的时候，是不会对他的反应感到惊讶的，他真的是值得相信的。当波妞为了展示魔法变回了小金鱼，他也没被影响，只是觉得波妞是一个很棒的小伙伴。宗介是一个很有趣的小男孩，从配音的效果能看出来，人们真的很喜欢他的表现——宗介对波妞的崇拜，不带任何偏见，他可以接受所有的事。随着故事的进展，然后你就想知道接下来他会遇到什么样的事情，他可以接受所有的事，但是对于我来说，他不会永远都那样。

AV：这部电影说的更多的是关于孩子之间的承诺，宗介答应会照顾好波妞。

HM：那确实很重要，但是一个人不会总是在他的世界里保持永远的真实，就好像你想保护一只小鸡，但是最后恰好是由于你过分的保护而使它死掉了。今天，当你长大后，你不得不学会不要遵守诺言，也就是说，在我的电影里，我想表现一个这样的小孩。

AV：你的意思是说，事物会随着人们长大而变化。

HM：我想像如果波妞去了幼儿园，她就会离开宗介而亲近 Kumilo。

AV：好惨呀！

HM：不必担心，也许对宗介来说，这可能是一种解脱，也可能不是。但是我觉得事情不会是那么简单，你可以想像等长大后宗介娶了波妞，但是生活不会是那么简单。

AV：谈到童年就涉及一些生命本质的东西，一些和我们自己的出生有关的东西，因此场景就会转到年轻父母。

HM：是这样的，对波妞来说是很难适应的。我想把她塑造成不断长大并逐渐追求完善的人，她的能力可以让她成功——这是一种与生俱来的力量。在影片中，她真的很关心小孩子，能同他们交流，但不是用语言。我知道那是人类先前所使用的交流方式。

简介

宫崎骏，生于 1941 年 1 月 5 日，是日本杰出的动画电影导演，也是吉卜力动画工作室的创建者之一。

他曾经历过一段默默无闻的日子，直到 1997 年米拉麦克斯电影公司上映了他的影片《幽灵公主》，该片使他在日本赢得了商业和评论家的认可，成为日本最赚钱的电影，不过这一称号被几个月后上映的《泰坦尼克号》取代。宫崎骏第一部赢得日本电影学院奖的动画影片是《千与千寻》，此片是首个赢得奥斯卡奖的动画电影奖，在票房上与《泰坦尼克号》

不相上下。《哈尔的移动城堡》也获得提名，但是最终未获奖。

宫崎骏的电影经常运用不变的人生主题，如人与自然及科技的关系，维护和平的艰难等等，他的电影通常都在票房收入上获得巨大成功，在这一点上甚至可以媲美迪士尼。2006年宫崎骏被时代杂志评为过去60年亚洲最具影响力的人之一。

Chapter 8 Henry Selick Talks about *Coraline*: The Electricity of Life 亨利·塞利克谈《鬼妈妈》——生命的激情

去年参观了《鬼妈妈》在波特兰的莱卡工作室的宏伟制作，最近又在焦点电影公司完整观看了这部真正意义的3D立体定格动画电影。上周终于有机会坐下来与导演亨利·塞利克一起回顾他的这部定格动画片制作过程。

比尔·德索维茨：让我们先从您在《鬼妈妈》的拍摄中使用的先进技术开始谈起吧，比如改良后的人物造型、可活动的部位零件、新材料的利用、真实毛发和布料质感的塑造、美丽的布景等方面；数字以及3D立体拍摄技术的应用是不是使角色更加富有质感、更加逼真？

亨利·塞利克：3D立体拍摄技术的运用确实在影片中占有很大的比重。在运用定格动画手段制作影片时，以及与其他制作方式进行对比时， 你必须知道各自的优点和缺点。对我来说，优点是那些都是真实的材料——缩小比例的角色和小道具，但这些东西都是真实存在的，并采用3D立体拍摄技术。我经常说我们没有最好的商业影片，但我们有最好的展览影片。因此人们可以来我们这里参观，看到这些种类繁多的微缩布景，森林和树木模型都用缆线一类东西控制，以便能在风中舞动，还有漂亮的灯光设计。这种感觉就像我们真正坐在电影院里观赏影片的体验一样。

BD：让我们谈一下影片中3D立体拍摄技术的运用，这在《鬼妈妈》的拍摄中是有着重大意义的。

HS：我运用3D立体拍摄技术有很长的历史，20年前我与连尼·利普顿为View-Master公司拍了3D立体岩石视频，连尼是现代数字3D立体电影的教父。

BD：你刚才提到View-Master，那正是我们称之为全新的“沉浸式”的3D产品。

HS：这可以追溯到那段时光：我遇见连尼的时候，发觉他真是个天才，我每隔几年就与他一起探讨3D立体拍摄技术的发展。回到拍摄《圣诞夜惊魂》和《飞天巨桃历险记》，在我们的团队中总有几个3D立体拍摄爱好者运用3D立体技术拍摄剧照。我们只是有这种渴望运用3D立体技术来拍摄定格动画。然后正是连尼，他建立了这种可能性，这正是《鬼妈妈》的漫长的孕育期，这期间开始拍摄定格动画和3D立体动画，这两个工作是同时进行的。最后，几年的时间，我一直希望将《绿野仙踪》拍成彩色版。但我想通过一种更加有独创性的方式，3D 立体摄影技术真的会让故事更有看头，于是将《鬼妈妈》带入了一个全新的世界， 最终我们把这部电影设计为 3D 立体电影，布景等形式都是为此特别设计的。

BD：幸运的是，我非常高兴地宣布大多数同事同意你的看法。杰弗瑞 · 卡森伯格说 3D 拍摄技术更多的是延续而不是打破。

HS：我很高兴人们有相同的结论。

BD：让我们来谈一下，在莱卡公司这个特殊的团队拍摄《鬼妈妈》的一些经历。

HS：找到优秀的定格动画制作团队成员真的不容易。定格动画并不是主流动画方式，我们的团队三分之一是在《圣诞夜惊魂》中或更早退役的人员。有些人在某种程度上已经与我共事 20 多年：玻 · 亨利，安东尼 · 斯科特，艾里克 · 雷顿。因此这部分成员已经知道如何相互交流。然后另外三分之一是当地的艺术家和来自俄勒冈州的波特兰的动画师。威尔 · 文顿的公司在制作定格动画尤其黏土动画方面有着悠久的传统。特拉维斯 · 奈特是我们的动画师领队之一，也是世界最好的动画师之一，是我合作过的前五名或者前十名的动画师，因此他把本地人才的标准定得很高。还有三分之一来自世界各地：许多英国人，加拿大人，比利时人，德国人，新西兰人。

BD：你以前提到你特意提醒大家要谨慎制作，力图达到完美。

HS：嗯，在过去，当雷 · 哈里豪森正在做他宏伟的定格动画怪兽，生物和电影特效，试图使它尽可能的真实，期望人们认为它们是真实的，并且他们做到了。但是到《侏罗纪公园》后情况变了，《玩具总动员》放映后情况又一次改变。我许多年一直在想，定格动画的优势是什么？我们应该努力坚持的是什么？它有许多优点：它是经由艺术家的手创作出的，你能感受到这一点。你可以感受到生命力量，但这是不完善的。它不能达到完美——而计算机动画恰好能弥补这一点。当影片突然演奏出绚丽的乐章，当所有的角色充满生机，我想这时观众会产生同样的共鸣——这就是生命的激情。

BD：关于定格动画您还有什么更深层的探索？

HS：话又说回来，问题是如何扬长避短。我觉得重要的是尽力保持主题。很多人担心太恐怖。我实际上回想运用迪士尼早期影片的方式来处理是非常有效的：比如《白雪公主》，《木偶奇遇记》，《小鹿斑比》，《幻想曲》。这种方法就是将《爱丽丝梦游仙境》与《格林童话》的探索相结合。一方面，我要回到传统的讲故事方式，它是尼尔 · 盖曼书的核心。但是，这次其他的动画师没有涉足这个领域，所以，对我来说是全新的探索。因此我内心所追寻的一部分是将定格动画带入新的领域：不再追随权威。我知道有很多其他方式，尤其是皮克斯的讲故事的方式，但那些电影的色调和感觉与我所想要的有很大的不同。

BD：您在找寻什么样的故事来讲述？

HS：对我并不是必要的，但我只是觉得动画可以做到这么多，《和巴什尔跳华尔兹》是我最想看的动画片。

BD：我迷上了它。

HS：你认为它怎么样？

BD：棒极了。

HS：瞧！我读到了它并且看到了一些图像。

BD：它确实给你留下很深的印象，它是如此刺激和风格鲜明。

HS：所以我知道它做对了，动画可以承担那样的主题。有些图画小说正在转变成真人电影，其中许多应该做成动画。有一件事情：特拉维斯 · 奈特正要运行一个那样的公司，他对制作 PG-13 级的动画片没有什么意见。那么我们为什么不做呢？如果我们找到或创作一个那样的故事，真是太棒了！也许大部分成功的真人实景电影是 PG-13 级的。我不明白为什么人们不愿承担更多的风险，就这一点回顾历史，抓住新事物的机会实际上是最好的办法。你永远也不会追上皮克斯，梦工厂，或蓝天工作室。他们都很好，只是他们太成功而不愿承担风险了。看看《机器人瓦力》，就会知道它彻底开辟了新的领域。制作适合家庭观看的电影是十分困难的，该片绝对是有开创新的。他们做得很不错，而我想做得更大胆一点，并且我们必须把成本降下来。

Chapter 9　Aardman Animation Studio　阿德曼动画工作室

阿德曼动画工作室，是一家曾获奥斯卡奖的英国动画公司，坐落于英国的布里斯托尔市（Bristol)。这家动画公司以其定格动画、黏土动画作品闻名于世，尤其是那对黏土版的老搭档——华莱士和阿高（Wallace & Gromit)。

彼得 · 罗德（Peter Lord）和大卫 · 史波克斯顿（David Sproxton）在上学的时候就开始了他们的动画合作。1972 年他们注册了一家名为“阿德曼”的动画公司。1976 年毕业后，他们搬到了布里斯托尔市，在那里他们为儿童节目创造了著名的动画人物——摩夫（Morph)。彼得和大卫在英国国家电影电视学校遇见了尼克 · 帕克（Nick Park)，当时他正在制作学生作品《月球野餐记》(*A Grand Day Out*)，1985 年尼克 · 帕克以全职身份加入了阿德曼公司。1986 年，英国音乐人彼得 ·盖布瑞尔（Peter Gabriel）提议联合导演斯蒂芬 ·约翰逊（Stephen Johnson）以及奎氏兄弟（Brothers Quay)，摄制一段新概念摇滚音乐电视作品《大锤》(*Sledgehammer*)，此片当年获奖无数。那种将节奏、激情、格调和独特视觉效果结合的创作方法，也被用在后来的妮娜 · 西蒙的著名单曲《我的宝贝只在乎我》(*My Baby Just Cares For Me*) 和罗伯特 · 帕克的《赤足而行》(*Barefootin*) 的视觉演绎之中。

1989 年阿德曼工作室再次受英国电视台第四频道委托，制作了五集（每集 5 分钟）系列影片《同期录音》(*Lip Synch*)，这些具有开创性的影片进一步探索了动画影片以真人角色和真实音效为基础的制作手法。此外运用这手法的作品还包括：彼得 · 罗德的《战争故事》(War Story) 和《有备而行》(*Going Equipped*)，巴瑞 · 普维斯的《下一个》(*Next*)，理查德 · 哥勒斯索斯基（Richard Goleszowski）的《识别》(*ident*)，尼克 · 帕克的《动物悟语》(*Creature Comforts*)。

1993 年，阿德曼工作室推出了尼克 · 帕克执导的其里程碑式的动画短片《引鹅入室》(*The Wrong Trousers*)，该作荣获奥斯卡最佳动画短片奖。这也是阿德曼工作室的首部 30 分钟的动画短片，世界范围的交口称赞和三十多个大小奖项让《引鹅入室》成为动画史上最成功的短片之一。1995 年，阿德曼工作室出品的《剃刀边缘》(*A Close Shave*) 为尼克 · 帕克迎来了第三座小金人。一系列的荣誉不仅为阿德曼工作室带来了声誉，也使"超级无敌掌门狗"(Wallace & Gromit) 系列故事家喻户晓。1996 年工作室乘胜推出了彼得 · 洛得执导的 11 分钟动画短片《双胞胎传奇》(*Wat's Pig*)，获得了当年奥斯卡提名。

1998 年，阿德曼工作室以影片《怯场》(*Stage Fright*) 获得英国学院奖（BAFTA）。这部 11 分钟动画短片，是受英国电视台第四频道委托制作。由尼克 · 帕克在《引鹅入室》和《剃刀边缘》中的主动画师史蒂夫 · 布克斯（Steve Box）担任导演一职。

阿德曼工作室第一部面向全年龄段的动画电视剧《小犬雷克斯》，由阿德曼的理查德 · 哥勒斯索斯基（Richard Goleszowski）创意并执导，于 1998 年首次在 BBC2 台播放，该剧获得了许多国际级的大奖。2001 年受 BBC2 委托，由戴伦 · 沃什（Darren Walsh）执导了该系列剧的第二部《愤怒小子》(*Angry kid*)，这是阿德曼第一部完全借由原子影业公司（atomfilm.com）网站发布的动画作品。

2000 年 6 月，阿德曼工作室与梦工厂合作的首部动画长片《小鸡快跑》(*Chicken Run*) 在美国和英国同期上映，此片由彼得 · 洛得和尼克 · 帕克共同执导，获得了舆论和票房的双丰收，在全球共获得 2.2 亿美元的票房收入。2002 年秋天，阿德曼工作室推出了"超级无敌掌门狗"系列的 10 集（每集 1 分钟）短片作品《疯狂发明》(*Cracking Contraptions*)，该系列短片首播于网络，浏览量数以万计，并于 2002 年秋季和圣诞节期间在 BBC1 台播出。作品同时通过原子影业公司的网站提供给美国的观众。

在良好口碑以及突出票房的感召下，由梦工厂发行的"超级无敌掌门狗"首部动画电影长片《人兔的诅咒》(*The Curse of the Were-Rabbit*) 于 2005 年 10 月上映。影片高居美国和英国两地票房成绩榜首，同时赢得了包括奥斯卡最佳动画长片（Best Animated Feature Film）以及英国学院奖最佳英国电影（Best British Film）等众多享有盛誉的国际大奖。

2006 年 11 月，阿德曼工作室首部 CG 动画电影《鼠国流浪记》(Flushed Away）由梦工厂发行上映，获得 2007 年英国学院奖（BAFTA）提名。2007 年 3 月，阿德曼工作室的电视动画《小羊肖恩》(*Shaun the Sheep*）于 BBC1 和 CBBC 首播，并在世界范围内销售。小羊肖恩的灵感来源于尼克 · 帕克 1995 年执导的奥斯卡获奖短片《剃刀边缘》。

“超级无敌掌门狗”系列的最新影片是《面包与死亡事件》(*A Matter of Loaf and Death*)，于 2008 年圣诞节在 BBC1 台播放，吸引了一千六百多万人的观看，获得了英国学院奖最佳动画短片奖。目前“超级无敌掌门狗”系列影片正在伦敦科学博物馆的一个重要展览中播出。阿德曼工作室首部为学龄前儿童制作的电视动画片《蒂咪时间》(*Timmy Time*）于 2009 年 4 月在 BBC 儿童频道（CBeebies）播出。

目前阿德曼公司正在与索尼公司合作两部动画长片：一部是动作冒险喜剧《亚瑟 · 圣诞》(*Arthur Christmas*)，预计在 2011 年的圣诞夜上映；另一部是《海盗——与科学家的一次冒险》，预计在 2012 年上映，其他影片正在筹备之中。从彼得和戴维的伏案创作开始到现在，阿德曼工作室已经成为一个世界级的重要动画机构，那些才华横溢、充满活力、具有责任感的阿德曼人将一如既往地呈现出充满创新性、趣味性和吸引力的作品。

Chapter 10　Te Wei and Chinese Animation 特伟与中国动画

为广大观众熟知的动画家特伟先生（1915.8.22—2010.2.4)，凭借着具有传统艺术风格的动画创作而成为中国动画的奠基人。他为中国动画付出了数十年的心血，作品获得国内外多项大奖，是中国唯一获得过国际动画协会终身成就奖的艺术家。

1956 年，执导影片《骄傲的将军》时，特伟在制片厂的墙上贴了一幅鼓励大家的标语，要求动画师们都能在创作中融入对民族精神的探索。《骄傲的将军》是中国动画第一次从京剧艺术吸取民族艺术精华的尝试。特伟说：“对于怎样从传统中借鉴有用的东西，我们有着清晰的思路——地方戏曲、戏剧艺术、京剧等都可以是灵感的来源，从其具有特色的造型动作中吸取了不少的养分。我们甚至还邀请到了剧团的老师来到制片厂亲自向我们展示表演中的动作技巧。

随着《骄傲的将军》的上映，其他带有浓厚中国风格的动画电影也在艺术界和社会上广泛流行，对动画的实验性探索加快，不仅在内容和技巧方面，在制作材料方面也有所突破。特伟说：“我们制作的剪纸动画以及木偶动画其灵感，都来自于博大精深的中国文化。我国的剪纸艺术和皮影戏有着悠久的历史传承，基于此，我们的剪纸动画探索十分成功。中国动画开创人之一的万古蟾与胡进庆合作，经过一年多的努力，制作出了中国第一部剪纸动画片《猪八戒吃西瓜》，并获得了奖项。

大约在 1960 年，特伟的动画风格受到国画大师齐白石作品的影响，拍摄了水墨动画电影《小蝌蚪找妈妈》(1960)，获得了五项大奖，包括昂西动画节、戛纳电影节和洛迦诺电影节等国际电影赛事；1963 年特伟创作指导了第二部水墨动画片《牧笛》；1988 年又以总导演的身份执导了影片《山水情》，在蒙特利尔国际电影节、上海国际电影节等赛事中获得五项大奖。1995 年国际动画协会授予特伟"终身成就奖"，特伟说："这个奖项意味着我可以在自己的艺术生涯中画上一个圆满的句号了"，他又解释说："我想我还可以为中国动画做更多的事情"。已经 86 岁高龄的特伟先生，仍然期待去导演一部更好的作品，那也许是一部水墨动画制作——因为在他心中，这项中国独有的技艺应该得以保存和发展。

1999 年，中国政府推选中国电影史一百部杰出影片，二十部动画片入选，特伟先生的作品有四部名列其中。作为中国动画事业的领军人物，特伟先生有三项伟大的贡献：

1. 创立了中国动画的民族风格；

2. 建立了一支高素质的动画制作团队：在他的领导下，上海美术电影制片厂从最初的几人发展到几百人的，在和万氏兄弟等老一代艺术家的通力合作基础上，又培养了年轻一代的动画精英；

3. 领导了包括中国动画黄金时期和大部分著名中国动画作品诞生时代的创作活动。

特伟访谈

Q：请您谈谈，在所有的中国艺术样式中，为什么水墨、剪纸、折纸、木偶等适用于中国动画的创作？

T：在 20 世纪 50 年代，我们认为应该制作有中国特色的动画片艺术，第一部动画片就是剪纸动画。那时候我们不把这些叫做卡通，而是叫"美术电影"。那时的创作人员很少提及我们是否应该从迪士尼学习，但是我们每个人确实很喜欢迪士尼动画的风格与动作技巧。动画具有很大的包容性，中国的剪纸、折纸、木偶等艺术也可融入其中，我们没有时间考虑它应该叫什么，我们首要的任务就是创作出具有民族精神的动画类型。我们也学习国外动画高超的制作技术。现在的问题是对外国动画的深入研究与探索不足。

Q：在您的人生经历当中让您最骄傲的事情是什么？

T：我的生命早已与动画艺术紧紧联系在一起，在这几十年里，我做了一件我认为十分重要的事情，那就是我一直在探索具有民族风格的动画方向。也许唯一能让人骄傲的事情就是我们在水墨动画艺术上做了一些前人没有过的实验。但是我很少因此得到满足，我总是觉得我的那些作品还存在着很多缺陷，每部影片完成后都会留下很多遗憾，这是很普遍的现象。那时候，电影公司对我们拍摄水墨动画给予了很多资金上的帮助，我们非常高兴能得到政府方面的有力支持。另一件事我想就是组织了一些有才能的动画人在一起工作。

Q：如果有机会的话，您还会在动画领域做哪些事情？

T：我对自己作品的要求十分苛刻，以前创作的时候，我很少关注观众的回应。这是我十分后悔的事情。如果有机会，我将竭尽全力做得更好。

Q：过去 50 年里，您认为动画艺术有哪些变化？

T：很难说产生了什么大的变化，艺术技巧一直在稳步前进，动画制作水平也进展顺利。在艺术上没有顶点和低谷。

Q：与其他国家相比，中国动画有什么样的特征？

T：从 1956 年开始，我就说过，中国动画应该在民族性上寻找自己的出路，直到我 1988 年退休都这么认为。其实这条路一直发展的比较顺畅，和其他国家的动画相比，有着独特面貌。1980 年以后，中国动画人参加了许多国际动画节，中国也有自己的作品获奖。这段时期，中国动画人开始有机会开阔自己的眼界，也逐渐发现他们自己的一些缺点。

通过这些国际性质的动画活动，国外同行有机会对中国动画有了更多了解。同时，中国动画人也向国外同行学习，通过对国外作品的观摩学习，中国动画人开始不再满足于仅仅创作传统风格的动画。他们知道应该学习更多的技巧，当然，收获长处的同时，不好的东西也乘虚而入。

Q：您认为从国外同行那学到了哪些东西？

T：在我们那个年代，动画人把更多的时间放在影片的创意探索方面。现在退休后，我发现一些动画人把精力转移到了为外国公司的加工制作上，那不应该是他们的工作，这样会对自己的创作产生不好的影响。这种现象已经持续有段时间了，不是最近才发生的事情，他们已经受到国外的影响。上海美术电影制片厂最近完成的《宝莲灯》，在市场方面取得了成功，你们或许在片中会看到一些迪士尼的影子。他们的努力是值得肯定的，最近几年已经很少能看到这样的影片了，能做出《宝莲灯》这样高质量的动画很不寻常。虽然在美学探索和氛围的塑造方面略显不足，在技艺和商业方面，此片是有贡献的。

我们不应该对一些影片期望过高，因为很少有动画师是把内在的热情注入创作当中。如今，世界范围内动画领域的竞争愈加激烈，中国动画人应该像制作《宝莲灯》一样迈开更大的步伐。迪士尼拥有自己的创作思路和方法，中国动画也应该有与众不同的创作方式，但是面对迪士尼和梦工厂等如此强大的公司，想超越是有些难度的。

Chapter 11 Richard Williams and *The Animator's Survival Kit* 理查德·威廉姆斯和《动画师生存手册》

理查德·威廉姆斯在举世闻名的影片《谁陷害了兔子罗杰》中的创造性的发挥，为他赢得世界动画界广泛声誉，他曾赢得过 3 项奥斯卡奖、3 项英国学院奖以及 250 个国际奖项。

在长达 50 多年的职业生涯中，理查德·威廉姆斯成为动画领域最具创新精神的导师之一，他的理念成功地将手绘时代和电脑时代的动画创作结合到一起。他的更为重要的贡献也许在于他将动画知识传递给后人，新一代的动画人前赴后继，将动画媒体推向了更新更广的领域。

20 世纪 90 年代，他为来自迪士尼、皮克斯、工业光魔（ILM）、太平洋数码（PDI）、梦工厂、华纳等世界各地工作室的动画师举办了“威廉姆斯动画大师班”。随后在 2001 年出版了极其畅销的专著《动画师生存手册》，总结了在动画创作史中总结下来的关于动画原理、方法、技巧等方面的真知灼见。这本书不仅对传统动画，而且对最新领域的动画制作都大有帮助。16 张 DVD 版的《动画师生存手册》，内容集合了他在大师班讲座的珍贵视频。

对威廉姆斯的赞美之词：

“可以说是当今最优秀的动画大师。”
《好莱坞报道》

“天才艺术家。”
（罗伯特·泽米吉斯）（《回到未来》，《谁害了兔子罗杰》，《阿甘正传》等影片导演）

“世界上最出色的手绘大师之一。”
《洛杉矶时报》

“国际动画界的领跑者。”
《纽约时报》

“被同辈人誉为‘动画师中的精英’。”
《观察者》

极端帧和细分帧（节选自《动画师生存手册》）

以摆动的钟摆为例：极端帧就是钟摆改变方向的地方，也就是方向改变时动作结束的地方。

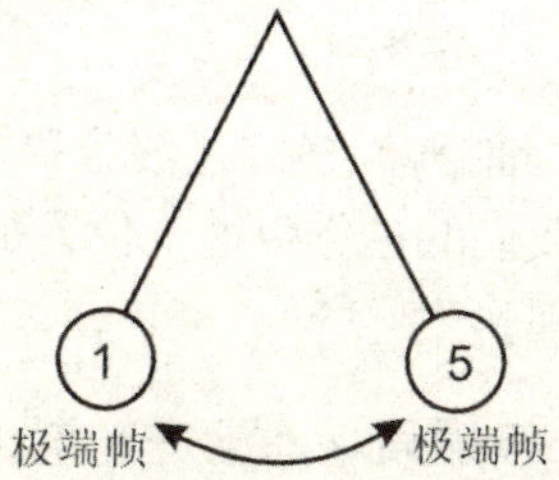

因为钟摆摆动时它的臂的长度不变，因此运动中的中间位置产生了弧线，从下面的图例可以看出两个极端帧之间的中间位置对我们是多么重要。

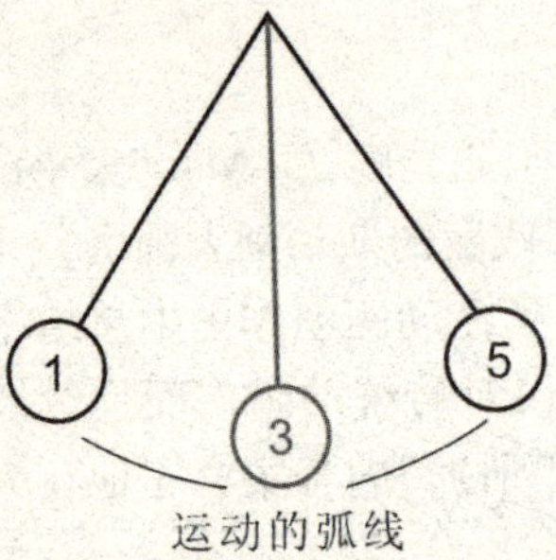

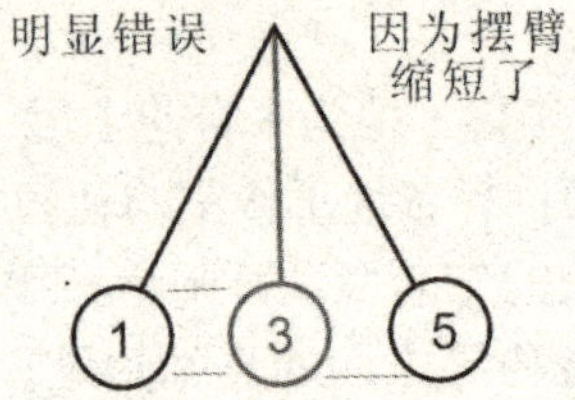

这个中间位置的重要性在此突显！在上个世纪三十年代人们称它为“细分帧”或“过渡位置”。

我们将在下面的图例中再加上两个中间帧。

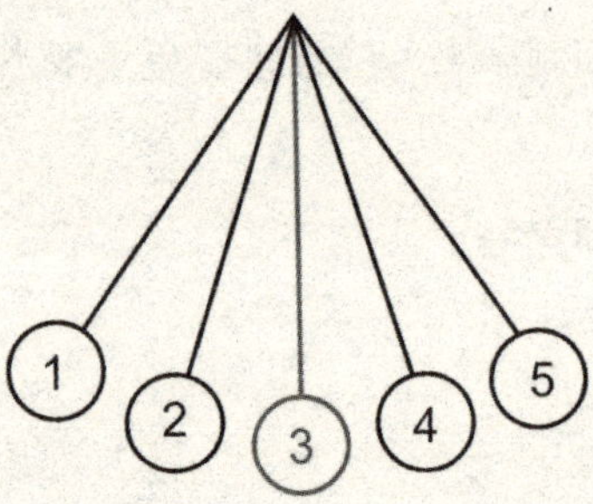

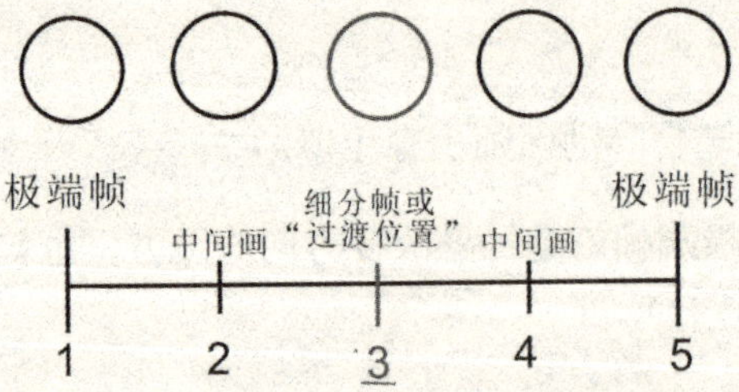

有的动画师会着重强调这个“细分帧”或“过渡位置”，因为它对于动作是至关重要的。我也有如此运用的习惯，因为在我们的创作中这个位置是制造生动效果的关键。我们将在本书后面各章节大量用到这个原理。

如果我们想要让钟摆在两个极端帧之间渐进和渐出，我们将需要增加中间帧：

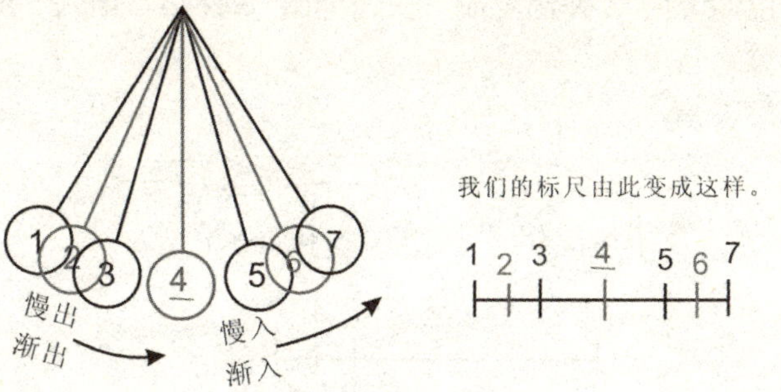

我们所要做的是让钟摆从极端帧渐入或渐出，“慢入”或“慢出”是传统的用词，但我更倾向于今天电脑动画师们的“渐入”和“渐出”的说法。

如果让钟摆的动作在结尾处放慢，我们就须再增加几个中间帧。

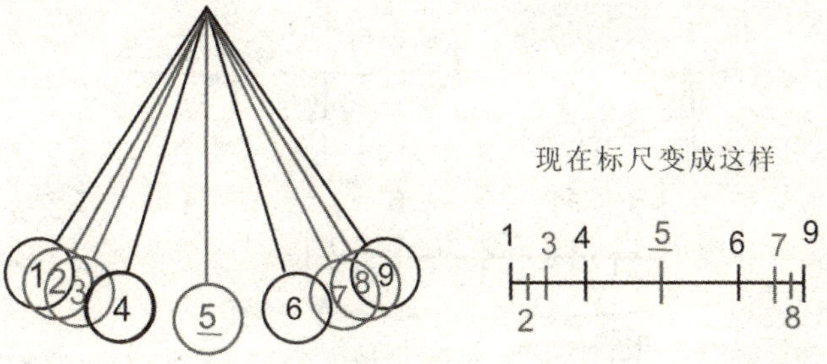

肯·哈里斯总是称它为“缓冲”，这是一个很好的表述。

迪士尼年轻创作团队的导师，动画奇才埃里克·拉尔森，认为动画应该更多体现形体的变化。那么就让我们从一只握着的拳头到伸出手指的变化过程开始：

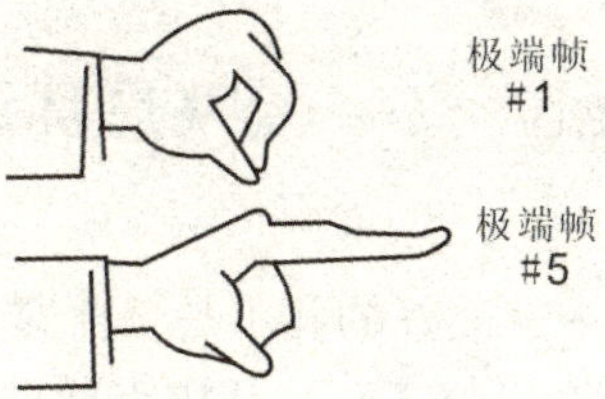

如果我们从 1 号极端帧“渐出”到指向 5 号极端帧，图示将会是：

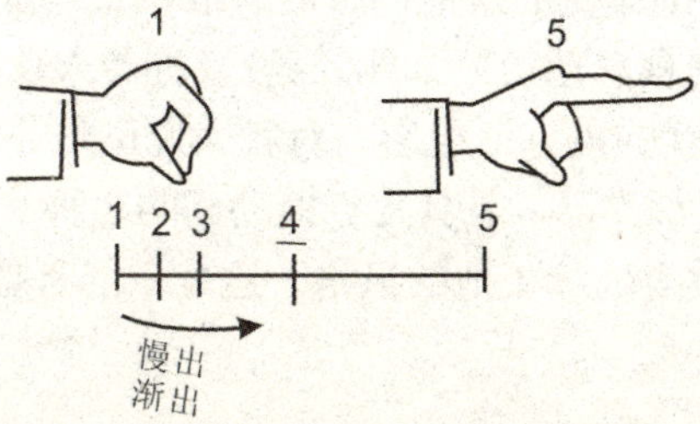

相反，如果我们攥紧的手“弹出”或“快速伸出”，然后“渐入”或“缓冲”到伸出的手指，图示将变成：

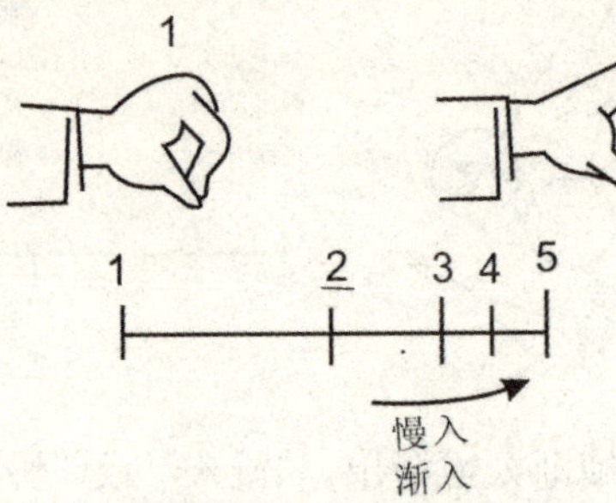

对于更轻松、缓慢的动作，我们就加入更多的中间帧和攥紧的拳头的渐出动作，在中间加速，然后再渐入到伸出的手指。

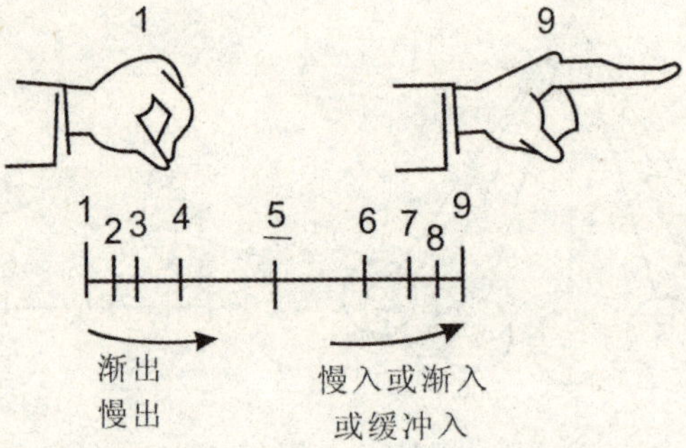

动画师可以只画两端的极端帧，接下来助理画师凭借这个标尺就会方便地把中间帧填进去。

Chapter 12　Movie Gallery：*Up*《飞屋环游记》

要从皮克斯的影片中挑选出一部最好的并不是一件容易的事情，因为每个人都有不同的标准。《玩具总动员》系列和《虫虫特工队》是皮克斯动画的开端，两者都非常有趣，和我们以前所看到的动画电影很不一样；《海底总动员》非常感人，并使得皮克斯动画工作室人气大增；《超人总动员》的制作完成是他们做过的最令人兴奋的一件事情；《汽车总动员》让我们感到温暖和怀恋；《美食总动员》如此经典；《机器人总动员》也非常独特。但是如果抛开最好而挑出一部最喜欢的皮克斯电影，对我来说倒是非常容易，那便是电影《怪物公司》。这是彼得·道格特首部作品，兼具皮克斯动画的各种品质，诙谐幽默，非常值得重复观看。《飞屋环游记》中彼得延续了他的风格，这是一部有趣、感人、令人兴奋、怀旧、经典、独特、诙谐幽默的电影。

卡尔·弗雷德里克森曾承诺和妻子过一种冒险的生活，但是这种承诺却被平平淡淡的生活所取代，尽管如此，他们依然生活得很幸福。当卡尔被迫搬出他和妻子共同生活了几十年的屋子时，他下定决心"带上"他深爱的屋子开始这场冒险之旅。然而，一个偷偷藏在飞屋里的小家伙、一只珍稀的大鸟和一个已经堕落的英雄，让卡尔的这次冒险之旅变得比预想的更加惊险。

《飞屋环游记》开头的10分钟也许是有史以来的动画电影中最精彩的10分钟，在让人感到温暖的同时又有几分心酸。皮克斯一直宣称将在每一部影片中开发一种新的技术以帮助他们实现一些效果（例如：苏利文的毛发和《海底总动员》中的水世界）。《机器人总动员》一定给予过这个创意团队相似的鼓舞，《飞屋环游记》的前10分钟几乎没有对话，这使得技艺表现得更加突出。与皮克斯的其他影片相比，《飞屋环游记》首先是一部充满想象力的电影，当小屋从我们身边消失，难以置信地悬浮在半空——当这一事实能够被观众接受的时候，其他一切也就变得顺理成章。幸运的是这一点在影片中并没有产生争议，或者是因为编剧的技巧，或者是因为这样的电影正好满足了观众的需求——任何原因都可能成立。一旦你度过了最初那段令人惊异的时间进而了解了影片中那些更具想象力的元素之后，接下来其他的内容就变得很自然了。

与其他制片厂的电影不同，影片笑料百出，但笑点并不依赖通俗文化所涉及的内容，或是存在于年轻人头脑中一些不合时宜的笑话。片中的幽默设置要优于皮克斯之前的其他任何影片。《飞屋环游记》真正的中心主旨是潜藏于影片里的，这一主旨是由故事的主角——一个名叫卡尔的老头引出的。皮克斯尽最大的可能将卡尔这一角色塑造成一个令人同情和真实可信的形象，使观众与卡尔这一角色在情感上产生共鸣。让观众关注一个从事简单工作且不需要付出太多努力的小角色，并不是一件容易的事，这类角色在好莱坞类型电影（实景真实电影或其他）从来不会作为主角出现，但《飞屋环游记》却毫不费力地把他搬上银幕。创作者们确实在幽默、故事和角色发展方面实现了超越，显示出才智。

《飞屋环游记》也许是皮克斯动画电影中拍得最美的一部。南美洲的仙境瀑布和数千只五彩气球，也许没有哪部影片能与如此优美的景致相媲美。影片中的角色设计并不是最新颖的，但对于本片来讲已经足够。卡尔本身是最成功的一个角色，从他粗暴的性格到缓慢的步伐，他的形象栩栩如生地展现在观众面前，吸引着观众关注他和他的故事。

在《迷失》、《超人总动员》、《星际旅行》等作品面世之后，迈克·吉亚奇诺便成为我喜欢的一位好莱坞作曲家，此次助力《飞屋环游记》，他再次以不同于以往但又一脉相承的风格显示出他的多才多艺。从怀旧情怀到激烈的情感，再到极度的冒险，吉亚奇诺从容地将剧作中的各个方面与音乐旋律实现了完美地匹配。

除了讲故事方面高超的能力之外，让皮克斯脱颖而出的可能还有在配音方面的出众表现。他们不愿意只寻找当下最红的明星来实现影片在票房上的影响力，而是抛开顾虑寻找最合适的声音来完成配音的工作。爱德华·阿斯纳的声音对于大家来说并不陌生，而他在本片中的出色表现超过了他在配音职业生涯中的任何一次，有评论认为这是他最完美的一次演绎。这是阿斯纳第三次也有可能是最重要的一次将角色融入生命的演绎。乔丹 · 长井扮演失去亲人宠爱的小探险家罗素，这一角色看起来有点儿小问题，也许是表演或角色设计方面所导致。或许让一个现实中小孩的本色出演要比雇来一个小主角“表演”更加真实。克里斯托弗 · 普拉默作为片中的反面人物非常胜任。联合导演兼编剧鲍德 · 彼得森证明了乔 · 兰福特（海姆里奇的配音和《虫虫特工队》的联合编剧）继续留在皮克斯的价值，乔 · 兰福特以歇斯底里的声音演绎了两只会说话的小狗道格和阿尔法。

导演彼得 · 道格特以其名下的两部最具喜剧性的电影奠定了其在皮克斯动画工作室的喜剧大王的地位。皮克斯动画以其动人的故事情节、卓越的动画制作技术以及真实的动画角色塑造，继续保持着他们在动画电影领域的一流地位。今年很难再有其他的动画电影能够超越《飞屋环游记》了。

Part 3 拓展篇

Chapter 13 Computer Animation Technology (1) 计算机动画技术(1)

计算机动画是指使用计算机制作动态图像的过程，通用术语中的电脑成像技术（CGI），既包括静态场景，也包括动态图像。计算机动画的独特性在于利用视觉暂留现象让一系列快速移动的图像变成动态画面。由于影像在视网膜上能够持续保持大约二十四分之一秒的时间，快速替换的图像造成了运动的假象。

尽管在风格化、低带宽的图像以及快速实时渲染等场合仍然使用二维计算机图形，但现代计算机动画通常采用三维计算机图形制作方式。有时动画的展示媒体是电脑本身，但有时目标媒体也可以是其他的形式，比如胶片等。

计算机动画本质上是基于三维模型的定格动画和基于二维图像的逐帧动画的数字化传承。为了制造运动的影像，图像被显示在计算机屏幕上，然后很快被下一幅图像代替。新图像和前面的图像相似，只是在此时间段内（通常的速度是 24 或 30 帧/秒）画面内容稍稍有一些改动。这种技术与电视或电影制造运动影像的原理是一样的。

对于三维动画，物体或者模型是在计算机中创建的，三维角色由虚拟骨架操纵。对于二维角色动画，使用独立物体或者图像以及相互独立的透明图层，有时也会用到虚拟骨架。接下来，动画师在关键帧上移动角色的四肢，眼睛，嘴巴，衣服以及角色的其他部分。计算机自动计算关键帧图像之间的外观差异，这也被叫做“补间”或者“形变”。最后，动画被渲染出来。

对于三维动画，所有帧必须在建模完成后才能渲染。对于二维矢量动画，在关键帧图像绘制的过程中就及时渲染了，而补间帧也是按需渲染。对于预先录制的图像，渲染帧被转换为不同的格式或媒体形式，比如电影或数字视频，这些帧也可能是在给终端用户呈现的时候实时渲染。通过互联网传送的低带宽动画（如 Flash、X3D）经常使用的客户端计算机安装的软件来实时渲染，而不是流媒体或预加载高带宽动画。

CGI 的历史

CGI 的首次使用是在 1973 年的《西方世界》（*Westworld*）中，这是一部科幻影片，影片描述了机器人与人类在同一社会之中生活、工作；而三维线框图像技术在 1976 年该片的续集《未来世界》(*Futureworld*) 中第一次使用，它使用了计算机生成的手和脸的虚拟图像，那是由当时犹他大学研究生艾德文 · 卡特姆（Edwin Catmull）和弗雷德里克 · 帕克（Fred Parke）制作的；第三部使用这种技术的电影是 1977 年的《星球大战》（*Star Wars*）；1979 年的《黑洞》（*The Black Hole*）使用了光栅线框模型渲染技术来描绘一个黑洞，同年的科幻恐怖电影《异形》（*Alien*）也应用了该技术，用来渲染太空飞船导航监视窗口这一镜头，按序排列的太空飞船沿信号灯塔的指引，降落在陌生的星球。

1978 年，纽约理工学院计算机图形学实验室的研究生们开始了当时第一部 CGI 电影长篇作品的创作，作品预告片在 1982 年国际计算机图形学年会（SIGGRAPH）上做了展示，但这部片子一直没有完成。在 1982 年 6 月首映的《星际旅行 2：可汗之怒》(*Star Trek II: The Wrath of Khan*) 中，展示了一组名为“创世纪（The Genesis Wave）”的计算机动画镜头。早期的两部投资巨大的影片《电子世界争霸战（*Tron*）》（1982）和《最后的星球斗士（*The Last Starfighter*）》（1984），运用了大量的三维计算机图形技术，电影在商业上的失败致使当时大多数导演开始拒绝使用计算机生成图像，甚至是看起来像是用计算机创建的图像也遭到排斥。“星际旅行系列”的另一部影片——1986 年的《星际旅行 4：抢救未来》(*Star Trek IV: The Voyage Home*) 中 CGI 技术的运用，即使在当时鲜为人知，但在接下来几年被证明是一个里程碑式的技术进步。

第一部将照片般逼真的 CGI 图像无缝集成到电影场景中的尝试是 1989 年的《深渊》（*The Abyss*），该片是由丹尼斯 · 穆伦（Denis Muren）和 詹姆斯 · 卡梅隆（James Cameron）执导的动作片，片中以五分钟的“假足”画面镜头而著称，这些触手是使用工业光魔公司（ILM）设计的新的突破性的算法技术制作生成。

Chapter 14　Computer Animation Technology (2) 计算机动画技术(2)

1991 年可以被认为是新 CGI 技术获得突破性进展的一年。两部大片《终结者 2：审判日》（*Terminator 2: Judgment Day*）和《美女与野兽》（*Beauty and the Beast*）都大量使用了

CGI 技术，这标志着好莱坞从逐帧动画和传统的视觉特效过渡到数字技术的开始。《美女与野兽》成为第一部获得获奥斯卡最佳故事片提名的动画长片，《终结者 2：审判日》荣获奥斯卡最佳视觉效果奖（Best Visual Effects）。

1993 年，另一部肯定 CGI 技术的电影《侏罗纪公园》（*Jurassic Park*）上映，片中利用 CGI 技术制作的恐龙与真人大小场景相结合的拍摄方式。CGI 提供了应用越来越广泛的完善制作工具。1994 年，CGI 技术被用来为《阿甘正传》制作特效，最值得注意的镜头是演员加里·西尼斯（Gary Sinise）腿的拍摄，运用了数字技术虚拟生成；其他特效还包括快速移动的乒乓球以及应用数字技术将汤姆·汉克斯的影像插入到几个历史片段回顾中。

1995 年，第一部全部运用计算机技术制作的动画电影长片——皮克斯的《玩具总动员》取得了巨大的商业成功。其他的数码动画工作室，如蓝天工作室、索尼动画公司相继开始制作数字动画电影。而原有的动画公司，如迪士尼公司，则开始由传统动画过渡到电脑动画的制作。

在 21 世纪初，CGI 成为影视特效的主要形式。摄像机跟踪软件的发明，有效地促进了视觉效果的丰富性，这是不可想象的技术进步；一个镜头的部分或全部背景的虚拟化制作成为电影制作中及其普遍的事情。

CGI 技术在电影中的运用通常渲染到约 1.4～6 兆像素，例如《玩具总动员》以 1536×922 分辨率渲染，就是 1.42 兆像素。渲染一帧的时间一般约为 2 到 3 小时，复杂的场景可能会花上数十倍的时间。这个时间在过去十年中基本没有多大改变，由于图像质量提高的速度与硬件的更新速度基本同步，不过更快的机器使得越来越多的复杂效果变得可行。随着图形处理芯片（GPU）处理能力和速度的增加，计算机中央处理器（CPU）的运算处理能力、存储速度和容量等方面的提升，这些在很大程度上增强了 CGI 的应用潜力。

CGI 技术的最新进展每年都会在国际计算机图形学年会（SIGGRAPH）中进行报道，SIGGRAPH 是一个计算机图形与交互技术的年度大会，每年数以万计的计算机专家参与其中。电脑游戏和 3D 视频卡开发者力争在个人电脑上获得实时的与 CGI 电影、动画质量相同的视频画面。

未来展望

就目前来看，三维电脑动画似乎可分为两类：仿真动画和非仿真（卡通式）动画。仿真电脑动画本身可以分为两个子类：照片级仿真动画和写实风格动画，照片级仿真动画在创造虚拟人物角色时应用了“表演捕捉技术”，也正是《最终幻想》（*Final Fantasy*）试图实现的。照片级仿真动画在将来最有能力给我们像《夜魔水晶》（*The Dark Crystal*）中那样的梦幻元素。而《蚁哥正传》（Antz）是一部写实风格动画的例子。虽然这些影片技术上不能堪称完美，但此类影片的创作水准仍然是不断进步的。非仿真动画或者卡通式动画更像是传统动画的延续，只不过是传统卡通动画的三维版而已，仍在使用和完善由迪士尼九大元老留传下来的传统动画的基本规律，比如基本的“挤压和拉伸”等。

Chapter 15 SIGGRAPH 国际图形学年会

35 年间，美国计算机学会计算机图形专业组（SIGGRAPH）从一个少数计算机图形学爱好者参与的社团，演变成了由研究人员、艺术家、开发人员、电影工作者、科学家等专业人士共同组成的大型学术团体，学会成员对计算机图形学和交互技术拥有着共同的兴趣。SIGGRAPH 的核心理念是卓越、诚实、热情、志愿者精神和强调交叉学科之间的互动。它不仅举办 SIGGRAPH 年度会议，还在世界各地城市开设地方分会，授予奖项给有突出贡献者，分享教育和网络资源，提议公共政策方案。SIGGRAPH 是 ACM（Association for Computing Machinery），即美国计算机学会的下属机构。

ACM 介绍

ACM 是世界上最大的教育性质的计算机科学学会，学会将教育工作者、研究人员和专业人士联合起来，促成相互间的对话与合作，共享资源并共同应对该领域的挑战。ACM 通过有效的领导力、高标准的专业提升能力和技术领域的卓越贡献来巩固其在计算机界的集体声誉。ACM 提倡其成员通过终身学习、职业培训和专业交流来实现自身的专业发展。许多 SIGGRAPH 的成员也加入了 ACM，成为其成员的有利之处在于可以自由获取全部 ACM 网上书籍和课程，得到机构职业就业中心发布的各种信息，同时可以通过订阅 ACM 电子邮件以获得专业科技新闻（TechNews）和职业新闻（CareerNews）等各种资讯。ACM 会员可以订阅数字图书馆（Digital Library）的内容，并可以访问在线计算机文献指南（Guide to Computing Literature），其特色是收集了一百多万种计算机领域的书目资料。

ACM SIGGRAPH 奖项

ACM SIGGRAPH 设立了为在计算机图形领域贡献终身的“考恩斯奖”；奖励有突出成就的“计算机图形成就奖”；为该领有技术创新和突破的专家而设立的“卓越创新研究学者奖”；还包括为出色志愿者颁发的“杰出服务奖”和在数字艺术领域取得成就的“杰出艺术家奖”。

DIGITAL ARTS COMMUNITY 数字艺术社团

ACM SIGGRAPH 数字艺术社区委员会致力于在国际组织间培育一个力量强大的数码艺术社区，并促进视觉艺术家和社区之间的交流。数字艺术社区委员会提供了一个互动艺术门户网站：arts.siggraph.org，以及与之相关的社区网络站点：siggrapharts.ning.com，为艺术家和科学家进行信息资源共享、艺术交流等提供方便。所有的SIGGRAPH成员利用该网站资源紧随艺术的最新发展、互相保持联系，并为找到合作者提供机会。

SIGGRAPH 年会

年会的亮点之一是它的动画剧场和电子剧场展映，展示许多最新上映的CG电影作品。在现场还设有一个大型的展览中心，数百家公司用精心布置的展位来吸引大家的眼球，同时招募新人。参展公司所涉及的领域包括工程设计、图形图像、电影和视频游戏行业，还有一些展位是为计算机图形艺术和交互艺术专业学校提供的。

每届年会上都会发表大量的研究性论文，SIGGRAPH由此也被认为是计算机图形学出版领域最负盛名的论坛，被SIGGRAPH接受的论文会在指定期刊《ACM图像处理》（ACM Transactions on Graphic）上发表，但发表的难度是很大的，最近的SIGGRAPH论文录取率一直低于20%。除了论文外，年会还设立了供业内专家进行各种主题讨论的版块，讨论话题包括计算机图形学、人机交互和教育等内容。会议期间，举办方还为参展人员提供了许多全日和半日制讲座，这些课程学习都是关于计算机图形学的最新进展。

自从1984年皮克斯的第一部动画短片《安德列与威利的冒险》在SIGGRAPH年会首映一炮而红，皮克斯成为在展会上发布最新作品的常客。

SIGGRAPH 亚洲会议

2008年以来，SIGGRAPH年会已经在亚洲举办了三次。第一次SIGGRAPH亚洲会议于2008年12月10日至13日在新加坡新达国际会议与展览中心召开；第二次是2009年12月16日至19日在日本横滨太平洋会展中心召开；第三次会议是2010年12月15日至18日在韩国首尔会议暨展览中心举行；第四次会议将于2011年12月12日至15日在中国香港召开。

Chapter 16 Academy of Motion Picture Arts and Sciences 美国电影艺术与科学学会

美国电影艺术与科学学会是享有盛名的国际电影组织机构，有超过6000余最杰出的电影专业人员参与其中。虽然世人对它的认识更多地是来自于一年一度的奥斯卡颁奖盛典，但是除此之外它还从事教育宣传、资料保存和学习研究等活动。学会的收入主要来自于每年一度的奥斯卡奖颁奖晚会电视转播节目的授权。目前学会的主席是汤姆·谢拉克。

美国电影艺术与科学学会设有许多研究机构，如玛格丽特 · 赫里克图书馆，它是世界上保存电影类研究资料最全最广的机构之一；电影档案馆则是保存电影作品、收集电影档案和为电影研究者提供资料的地方；科技委员会旨在提供讨论电影业和娱乐业协调发展的论坛，收藏电影科技史资料。学会安排了很多非盈利的公共活动，如电影回顾展、系列讲座和展览，全年的活动日程排得非常紧凑。学会还资助某些电影组织，以促进其发展。学会还负责指导在校学生，鼓励他们通过电影来表达自己的创意。

设施

美国电影艺术与科学学会的各个管理机构大多设在洛杉矶市的三个办公地点：位于比弗利山庄的总部大楼，是专门为学会而设的；另外两个电影研究中心，一个在比弗利山庄，另一个在好莱坞。好莱坞电影研究中心是改扩建而成，包括图书馆、电影档案馆和其他的机构。比弗利山庄的总部大楼里有两家免费向公众开放的画廊，一个是位于底层的大厅画廊，另一个是位于四楼的画廊，经常举办各种不同的电影及电影人物展览。

塞缪尔 · 戈德温剧院能容纳 1012 人，有先进的专用信号发射设备和音响系统，可提供一流的电影播放效果。位于总部大楼的剧院每年的公共演出日程安排得十分紧凑，包括会员专场、电影首映式和其他特别的活动（如每年一月电视现场转播奥斯卡颁奖礼）。同时还有能容纳 67 个座位的小剧场和位于碧克馥电影研究中心大楼内可容纳 286 人的林伍德 · 邓恩剧院。此外还有一个专门用来举办纽约地区的活动的剧院，设在在灯塔国际中心。

会员

学会成员是受主管委员会的邀请加入，评判的资格为是否曾经获得过奥斯卡奖的提名；也可由那些为电影业的发展做出过杰出贡献的人士提名成为会员。

新会员的选举提案每年进行一次，那些受邀新加入会员的名单会通过新闻发布会公布，但是学会不公开其全部会员的名字。所有的会员被分在十五个代表不同电影学科的分部里，每个会员只可以在一个分部工作。除此之外还设有自由会员，其成员拥有与分部会员相同的特权，但是不能派代表进入主管委员会。

另外设有附属会员，可以和内部各单位保持紧密的联系，但他不能参与电影的制作。其成员们既不能进入主管委员会，也不能参加学院奖的投票。

学会的专业分布

演员

艺术总监

电影摄影

导演

纪录片

执行官

电影剪辑

化妆和发型设计

音乐

制片

公共关系

短片与长片动画

音效

视觉效果

剧本

Chapter 17 California Institute of the Arts 加州艺术学院

迪士尼在他的回忆录中写道："年轻艺术家们需要的是一所能学到各种技能的学校，一个可以互相交流知识的地方。只要付诸努力，在任何领域都可能创造奇迹，这是促使人不断向前的动力。代表人类发展进程的艺术家们必须适应不断的变化，才能保持他们的社会价值和社会影响力。音乐家的天赋、演员的表演才能、出色的艺术家的技巧正在越来越多地应用于今天的商业发展——不但是他们自己，还有彼此领域之间相互合作产生的价值。所以我们需要的是一个培训艺术家的全新方法，一个全新的教育理念，它能够培养真正的艺术家，让他们拥有工作中不可或缺的重要技能——创造力和表现力。对于专业学校来说，不仅能提供给学生专业的教育，而且应在更广泛的知识背景下传授艺术表现的方法。正是为了满足这个需求，加州艺术学院才应运而生，这也是我们如此强调教学方法的重要性的原因。学生可以在这里学到各个方面的知识，包括美术、戏剧、音乐、舞蹈、写作等技能，毕业后将获得美术学士学位。在校学生的人数不应该超过两千人，并且尽可能让他们住在学校。学校会为表现突出的学生提供各种补贴，让他们可以把精力集中在艺术创作上，让他们可以自由表达。学校将会设立多种形式的奖学金制度，使学子们可以减少学业之外的压力。我们不需要浅尝辄止的业余爱好者，我们需要的是有才能和潜质的人。进入加州艺术学院学习的唯一条件是：才华。能为以后的年轻人提供发展其才能的地方，我想我们已经开始。”

加州艺术学院通常也被简称为“CalArts”，坐落于加州洛杉矶的瓦伦西亚，成立于 1961 年，是美国创意教育领域最早授予学位的高等学校，致力于视觉艺术和表演艺术的培养。

华特 · 迪士尼于 20 世纪 60 年代初期创建了加州艺术学院，师资力量雄厚，它实现了迪士尼在教育领域的梦想——建立一所像加州理工学院那样各学科间能相互融通的艺术学校。加州艺术学院为各领域艺术家提供相互合作的环境，学生们可以在工作室自由地发挥他们的创作潜质，每个人的想法都能受到整个团队的尊重；在这里传统权威不断受到挑战，教师从不采用灌输式的教学方法，而以启发方式取而代之。不同文化背景艺术家之间的交流有助于更好的艺术实践，从而在更广阔的空间里取得艺术的进步。

加州艺术学院下设有许多可提供各种层次学位的专业学院：美术学院、人文学院、舞蹈学院、影视学院、音乐学院和戏剧学院。其中影视学院是美国影视专业最杰出的学院之一，它不遗余力地致力于将影视作为一个独立艺术形式的探索。这所学院的与众不同之处是它的专业包括了最主要的影视类型：戏剧编导、纪录片、角色动画、实验动画、多媒体和装置艺术。课程设置有四个部分具有挑战性的教学计划，每一个都有自己的特色。这种课程训练体现了“严谨的实际训练和理论研究相结合，动手能力和美学修养相结合”的教学思想。在加州艺术学院毕业著名的校友有蒂姆 · 伯顿（79 届角色动画专业）、约翰 · 拉斯特（79 届角色动画专业）和亨利 · 塞利克（77 届实验动画专业）。

Chapter 18 Japan Animation Industry Trends 日本动画产业的发展

概述

日本动画业蜚声世界。在电影、电视及录像制作业不断拓展国内市场的时候，日本动画业早已开始将眼光瞄向了国外市场。与此同时，新的电影筹资方式也应运而生，在这样的背景下，日本动画产业正在努力解决专业人员短缺、国内电影制作单位减少的缺陷，迎接拓宽国外市场的挑战。

市场纵览

2004 年日本动画业的话题是 11 月上映的宫崎骏导演力作《哈尔的移动城堡》，此片由吉卜力工作室历时三年制作完成。观影人数在短短的 44 天里就超过了 1000 万，其上座速度超过了日本以往任何一部电影，之后这部电影一直热映不衰，截止到 2005 年 3 月 8 日观众人数增长到1423万，打破了宫崎骏的另一部作品《幽灵公主》所创下的票房纪录，并取代它成为日本电影史上票房排名第二的影片。《千与千寻》于2003年获得第75届奥斯卡最佳动画长片奖，这是该片在2002年赢得柏林电影节金熊奖之后再一次获取殊荣，又一次证明了日本制作国际水平动画电影的生产能力。2004年，导演押井守的动画电影《攻壳机动队2》获得戛纳电影节提名，该片是《攻壳机动队1》的结局篇，曾名列美国《公告牌》杂志榜首。

然而，要享誉全球，日本动画产业还需充分端正其姿态。在前行的过程中，日本动画产业在拓展海外市场的同时，还必须通过发展主要产品的分销系统和培训专业人员，来抓住动画产业的全球商机。虽然制作体系实际上已经建立起来了，但是动画产业仍在国内外市场分布和维权方面有很多明显的弱点，比如许可权、一般的国际商务知识等。在人员发展方面，动画设计师并没有享有与之相适应的社会地位，因此日本的动画人才都转向其他行业和国家，这也是一个严重的问题。

市场份额分布

日本国内动画市场广义上可以大致分为三类：

1）动画长片电影

2）电视节目

3）以上内容的声像版产品以及原创作品

根据日本媒体发展研究所的统计，2003年日本动画市场销售额是1912亿日元，包括动画电影的票房收入、电视动画产品收费以及声像制品的销售和出租收入，同比下降了10.4%，这是两年来的第一次下降（见图一）。2001和2002年之所以能有如此可观的收益很大程度上是由于2001年《千与千寻》在票房上的成功（304亿日元）以及2002年DVD版的销售收入。而2003年由于缺少像《千与千寻》这样重量级的作品，所以导致了市场的萎靡，但据估计，由于动画电影《哈尔的移动城堡》的成功上映，销售额将在2004年有所增长。

动画市场的价值大约有两万亿日元，内容包括动画形象授权、动画周边产品及动漫玩具等。

附录Ⅱ：常用动画术语表

ACADEMY AWARDS 奥斯卡金像奖：美国影艺学院于1927年设立的奖项，每年颁给表现杰出的电影工作者。每一个奖项最多有五个提名。

action 动作：动画角色从进入舞台到退出舞台所做的移、转、跳、跑等各种姿态。ACTION在电影中为“开拍”，为导演用来命令演员开始表演的口头用语。

adaptation 改编：将故事、小说、戏剧或其他适合透过电影、动画媒体来处理的作品搬上银幕。

animated feature 全长动画：90分钟以上长度的动画。

animatic 动态故事板、动画预演：为了让导演和动画师对故事本身进行审查，将故事板按时间分配及顺序对故事板进行动态影像化并制作出样片的过程。

animation camera 动画摄影机：一种装有停顿马达的摄影机，可单格拍摄，拍摄时装在动画摄影台上，可垂直移动，以改变被摄影的影像大小，或产生变焦的效果。

animation film 动画电影

animator 原画师、动画设计者：相对于中间画师(inbetweener)时为原画师，其他情况基本为动画制作者的通称。

antic(anticipation)预备动作、动画预期：让观众能够产生“预期性”或者让观众预知角色的下一步动作。

anticlimax 反高潮：在电影最后解决冲突时，没有出现观众所期待的情节，使观众感到失望的情节设计效果。

antihero 反英雄：电影、戏剧或小说中的一种角色类型。他们富有同情心，但以非英雄的形象出现，通常对社会、政治和道德采取冷漠、愤怒和不在乎的态度。

art direction 美术设计：为影片造型进行设计和制作。

assistant animator 助理动画师：在主动画师(lead animator)的带领下进行关键帧的绘制。

asynchronism 音画分离：指影片上的声音和影像不相符。有时是为了特别的表现意图而刻意为之。

atmosphere sketch 气氛草图：确定影片场景气氛的草图。

B．P．(bot pegs)下定位：定位孔或者定位点位于动画纸下方的定位方法。

background(BG)/foreground：动画背景/前景

BRK DN(B．D．)(break-down)中割、受控制帧：是一种特殊的关键帧，它与临近关键帧在时间上保持一定的比例关系。BREAKDOWN 在电影中为“支配表”，指依场景和天次列出影片拍摄时所需事物的明细表。

C．U．(close-up)特写：影视动画或者摄影艺术中的一种镜头景别，拍摄人脸或者物的一部分，使特别放大。

camera angle 摄影机角度

camera movement 摄影机运动：指电影摄影机的运动，目的在于跟随一个动作，或改变被摄场景、人物或物体的呈现方式。

camera shake 晃镜头：晃动镜头技巧是指拍摄过程中摄像机机身做上下左右前后摇摆的拍摄。常用作主观镜头，如在表现醉酒、精神恍惚、头晕或者造成乘船、乘车摇晃颠簸等效果，创造特定的艺术效果。

camera tracking 摄影机追踪：摄影机跟踪功能可能轻松地捕捉实拍时摄影机的运动轨迹，这样虚拟摄影机就可以将三维造型逼真地“放置”在实景中。

CEL/celluloid 赛璐珞、透明片、电影胶片材料：用以附着感光药膜的透明片基，通常是用硝酸纤维等原料制成。

character-based animation 角色动画

character arc 角色性格曲线：体现为在故事变化过程中，角色人物最终克服各种局限，使得情境发生改变。

claymation 黏土动画：定格动画的一种，它由逐帧拍摄制作而成，它是用黏土或橡皮泥等可塑材质来制作人物，一般运用金属骨架来控制角色的造型和姿态。

clean-up 清稿：是手绘动画制作流程中的一个部分，主要对通过铅笔稿审查的动画进行清理和重新临摹,使画面更为统一。

click track 节拍音轨：在录音时，一个专门用来播放滴答声，作为和录音者之间同步的依据。

climax 高潮：指戏剧或电影故事发展中，情绪张力最强的时候，通常一部电影或戏剧故事均有一个或一个以上的高潮。

color flash(paint flash)跳色

color keys=color mark-ups 色指定

composer 作曲：负责为影片编写和安排音乐内容的专业人员。

composition 构图：绘画时根据题材和主题思想的要求，把要表现的形象适当地组织起来，构成一个协调的完整的画面。

computer generated imagery(CGI) 电脑影像合成技术：是计算机数字图像(computer graphics，简称 CG)在影视特技领域的应用。

concept drawings 概念图：将电影场景中的动作进行视觉化的草图方案，可以为团队提供准确思路。

conflict 冲突：是一切剧作的基础，为人物规定出需求，即在剧本中确立他想要达到什么目的后，就可以为这一目标的实现设置障碍，这样就产生了冲突。

cross in/cross out 入镜、出镜：指演员自画面的一边进场或朝画面的一边出场。

dialog (dialogue) 对白及口形

director 导演：影视制作团队的领导者，负责把握整部影片的演绎手法、视听风格和动作节奏。

dissolve(X. D) 溶景，叠化

distortion 变形

double frame 双(画)格

double image 双重影像

draft 草稿，草图

drawing disc 动画圆盘

dubbing 配音

dwf(drawing) 画，动画纸

E. C. U = extreme close up 大特写

ease-in 渐快、淡入：角色由静止到运动作加速运动。

ease-out 渐慢、淡出：角色由运动到静止作减速运动。

editing 剪辑

editor 剪辑师：负责将影片单个镜头或者段落编辑链接工作的人员，电影蒙太奇组合阶段负责剪接影片的人。

EFT(effect) 特效

enter(in) 入画：指动画人物或者角色进入摄像机可视范围，在镜头中出现。

episode 片集： 一段故事情节或插曲

exit(moves out, O. S.) 出镜、退场：指动画人物或者角色退出摄像机可视范围，从镜头中消失。

experimental animation 实验动画：指非商业的探索性质的动画作品。

exposure sheet(X-SHEET)摄影表：即律表，它是导演对脚本上每一个镜头按时间顺序所做的摄影指示的一种表格，它是原画设计动作的参照，也是最后剪辑、合成的依据。

EXT(exterior) 外面、室外景

fade(in/on) 画面淡入：镜头内容由黑场或者完全透明过渡到正常样式。

fade(out/off) 画面淡出：镜头内容由正常过渡到黑场或者完全消失。

field(FLD) 安全框：防止字幕或者人物做动作时偏出镜头中心范围的指示框。

flipbook 翻页动画书、动画手翻书

focal length 焦距

frame 格、帧画面

frame by frame 逐帧动画：采用传统动画的制作方式，把要表现的动态分解成一个个的动作，然后逐帧绘制，最后连续播放时形成动画效果。

freeze frame 停格、画面冻结

gag 笑料：动画中主要依靠人物的形象、夸张的表情、肢体动作等来制造笑料。

hook up 接景、衔接：将两张或者多张过大的背景或者其他画面分开绘制，然后再将其衔接。

I&P(ink & paint) 描线和着色

inbetweener 中间画动画师

key animator 关键帧画师：在一些成本较高的动画作品中，主要角色的动画将会由动画师组成的专门小组来完成。小组由一个动画监制(SUPERVISING ANIMATOR)、主动画师(LEAD ANIMATOR)和助理动画师(ASSISTANT ANIMATORS)组成。

key frames 关键帧：关键帧相当于传统手绘动画中的原画，指角色或者物体运动变化中的关键画面。

keys 原画：动画片中交代运动中人物或物体的主要动态之画片如起步、停止，或变换方向，通常关键动态由动画设计负责绘制。

layout 设计稿、动画设计方案：在工作性质上接近中文的"构图"。指动画影片中人物和背景的造型设计，也指负责这个工作的人。

limited animation 低成本动画：在卡通动画制作过程中，整个影片出现的共同影像，可以在画面中重复使用。

line test(pencil test) 铅笔稿试拍、线拍

lip sync(synchronization) 对嘴、唇形对位：指对白与演员的嘴唇动作达到精确的同步效果。

live action (和动画电影相对应的)真人与实景电影

M. C. U. (mediium close up) 近景

M. S. (medium shot) 中景

MAG TRACK(magnetic sound track) 音轨

model sheet 角色设计：动画影像分镜(ANIMATIC)获得通过后，故事板将会分发到设计部门按故事内容进行具体设计。角色设计工作有时是和故事板同时进行的，并制作出设计图。

montage 蒙太奇：一种处理空间与时间的艺术手段，是电影制作过程中决定影像时空的中心技巧。

morphing 形变动画：就是由一种形状变形为另一种形状的动画。

mouth charts 口形图

N．G．(no good) 不好的，作废

O．S．(off stage off scene) 出景

off model 走型

OL／UL(underlay) 前层与中层间的景

OL(overlay) 前层景、覆盖图

out of scene 到画外面

overlap action 重叠动作

P．T．(painting) 着色

paint flashes(color flashes) 跳色

palette 色板：绘图软件中可以选择颜色的调板。游戏和网格动画中可以使用的颜色通常极为有限。

pan 移动、平移

papercut 剪纸片：由中国剪纸艺术衍生的一种动画种类。

peg bar 定位尺

pencil test 铅笔稿试拍、线拍：在制作场景动画时，原画师(ANIMATOR)通常会对该场景中的动画进行一次铅笔稿的试拍(PENCIL TEST)，线拍是一个动画场景最终形态的初期形式，类似于一个样片。

performance capture 表演捕捉技术：以三维特效的形式将多名演员的面部表情及肢体行为真实的再现。

persistence of vision 视觉暂留现象：物体快速运动的影像在人眼中仍能继续保留一小段时间，是动画、电影等视觉媒体形成和传播的最基本的原理。

perspective 透视

pixilation 实体动画：以人或实物为拍摄材料的一种动画影片。

post-synchronized sound 后期同步录音

producer 制片人：制作团队的关键成员，负责确保影片在限定的时间和预算范围内进行制作，并从导演的角度支持项目制作，与投资方和发行商谈判所有的发行及相关事宜。

production designer 美工师：又称“美术设计”，主要工作任务是统筹设计安排全剧的布景、服装、化妆、道具，设计全剧的、每场戏的、每个培养的色彩基调。

protagonist 推动故事往前发展的主要角色：这一术语常与明星、英雄交换使用。

puppet 木偶片：以木偶角色形象表现故事情节的美术影片。

re-peg 重新定位

registration holes 定位洞

registration pegs 定位器

rendering 效果图，渲染

S．S(screen shake) 画面振动

SC(scene) 镜号、场、场景：由单一镜头或数个镜头组成的戏剧单位。通常包含全部故事要素的视觉范围，包括开端、发展和结局。

scene planning 场面调度：指对剧场的舞台上一切视觉元素的安排。

science-fiction film 科幻片:电影类型的一种，其特色的情节包含了科学奇想。

script 脚本：通常记载台词、对话和动作等信息，是使故事脚本或小说详细化的工作，可具体到人物的对话、场景的切换、时间的分割等等。

secondary action 伴随动作：依附在主要动作之下的细微动作。

self-line(self-trace line) 色线

sfx(sound effect) 声效、音效

shadow 阴影

shadow puppetry 皮影戏

sheet timer 时间设定：在分镜设计进行的同时，时间设定导演(TIMING DIRECTOR)将会通过分析动态故事板(ANIMATIC)来控制时间，角色的姿势和嘴型将被具体分配到各个帧，然后制作摄影表(exposure sheet)。

shot 镜头：摄像机不间断拍摄的一组帧序列，它常被看成一部视频的最小结构单位。

silhouette(silo) 剪影：以黑白二色形成的正式图像的“影子”，常用来判断动画片画面、动作表述是否清楚。“剪影片”是一种类似于“剪纸片”的动画类型。

size comparison 大小比例

slow in 慢进：静止的物体开始移动时由慢而快。

slow out 慢出：将要停止时的物体则会由快变慢。

special effect 特效：不是以直接的电影拍摄技巧获取的镜头。包括需要使用轮廓遮幕、多重影像蒙太奇、分割银幕、画面渐量、模型等技巧的镜头。也应用于爆破、弹道效果和机械效果。现在另外一个影视特效实现的途径是利用计算机软件来生成。

speed line 流线、速度线：在动画中表现运动物体，往往在其后面加上几条线来代表快速运动的物体，就是利用这种感觉来强化运动效果，这些线称之为速度线。

spin 旋转

staging 演出布局：仔细设计安排动画中的构图、运镜、动作、走位，避免在同一时间又过多琐碎的动作与变化。

stop-motion 定格动画：也称停格动画或逐格动画，是一种以手工制作的人物模型为对象，应用摄影技术来制作的一种动画形式。

storm out 速转出

story editor 剧本编审：电影公司编剧部门的职员，职责在审阅故事大纲，并对读稿员所提供的戏剧或其他文字材料加以评估。

storyboard(SAB) 分镜头台本、分镜头脚本、画面分镜剧本：以草图、绘画或照片，依连戏顺序将影片段落或整部影片的主要动作和叙述流程摘述出来。广泛地被用在动画片的制作，以及呈给客户审阅的电视广告影片企划中。

streaming 流媒体：指对网络视频、动画等多媒体文件边下载边播放的流式传输方式。

stylist 样式设计师，造型师

T．A．(top aux) 上辅助定位

T．P．(top pegs)上定位：定位孔或者定位点位于动画纸上方的定位方法。

texturing 材质贴图

theme 故事的主题：动画中所表达出的价值观，如宽恕、复仇、友谊、环保等主题。

three-act sructure 三幕结构：指的是剧本的结构，包括开端、中段和结尾三部分。

timing 时间选择与控制

tittle 片名，字幕

TR(trace) 描线

transition 转场：自一场景转至另一场景，或自一段落转至另一段落时，所采用的种种方法。

treatment 影视剧的情节大纲：在前期策划阶段用于陈述导演关于影片纲要的文件。

truck in 镜头推入

truck out 镜头拉出

tweened frames 补间帧：在补间动画中，由计算机自动运算并补齐的中间帧。

tweening 补间动画：在基于关键帧的动画制作法中，由计算机自动运算并补齐的中间帧动画。

UL(underlay) 中景、后景

V.O. (voice over) 旁白、画外音

vector 矢量：计算机显示的图形一般分为两类——矢量图和位图。矢量图与分辨率无关可无限放大不失真。

vert up 垂直上移

visual effect (VFX) 视觉特效：是影视制作领域一种通过创造图像和处理真人拍摄范围以外镜头的各种处理方式。通常涉及真人镜头和计算机生成图像(CGI)的合成以创造虚拟的真实场景。

voice director 声音导演

wipe 转(换)景方式

wire-frame 线框建模：线框建模生成的实体模型是由一系列的直线、圆弧、点及自由曲线组成，描述的是物体的轮廓外形。

work print 工作样片

X(X-DISS) (X. D.) 两景交融

X-sheet 摄影表

xerox down 缩小

xerox up(xerox paste-ups) 放大

zoom chart 镜头推拉轨迹

zoom in 推进

zoom lens 变焦距镜头

zoom out 拉出

Reference 参考文献

◎**Animation Writing and Development: From Script Development to Pitch**

Author: Jean Ann Wright

Publisher: Focal Press; First Edition edition (2005)

◎**The Illusion of Life: Disney Animation**

Author: Ollie Johnston

Publisher: Disney Editions; Rev Sub edition (1995)

◎**Animation from Pencils to Pixels: Classical Techniques for the Digital Animator**

Author：Tony White

Publisher: Focal Press (2006)

◎**Creating 3-D Animation----The Aardman Book of Filmmaking**

Author：Peter Lord，Brian Sibley，Aardman Animations

Publisher：HARRY N. ABRAMS INC. (1998)

◎**Animation in Asia and the Pacific**

Author：John A. Lent

Publisher：Indiana University Press (2001)

◎**The Animator's Survival Kit**

Author：Richard Williams

Publisher：Faber & Faber(2001)

◎**Enchanted Drawings: The History of Animation**

Author：Charles Solomon

Publisher：Random House Value Publishing (1994)

◎**80 Years of the Oscar: The Official History of the Academy Awards**

Author：Robert Osborne

Publisher：Abbeville Press (2008)

◎**Industrial Report (C) JETRO Japan Economic Monthly, June 2005**

◎**To Infinity and Beyond!: The Story of Pixar Animation Studios**

Author: Ķaren Paik

Publisher: Chronicle Books (2007)

网站：

www.animatedviews.com

www.awn.com

www.calarts.edu

www.fi.edu

www.wikipedia.org

后 记

随着现代教育的不断深入发展，专业英语教学始终是文理各领域学科关注并研究的热点问题。近年，国内很多影视、动画院系也相继开设了影视动画英语课程作为专业选修课，有些学校已将之设置成为必修课程。这正是当代社会对人才素质要求越来越全面的体现，也是动画教育面对国际交流的必然趋势。这种变化既要求影视动画专业的毕业生拥有扎实的基本功训练，同时又能运用外语这一工具获取专业信息，具备能够和国际同行进行专业交流的能力。

到目前为止，我们已经为数届动画专业的本科生开设了此课程，为了找到一种适应艺术类学生特点和要求的专业英语教学方法，我们邀请了英语、影视动画和美术专业的几位教师共同合作，深入课堂实践，总结其他院校的优秀经验，在英语知识和艺术专业技能两方面反复研究、修改，出版了这本教材。它力求知识点全面，语言鲜活、准确、流畅。

作为教师，笔者深知开设这样一门课程存在着相当的难度。有了领导的支持和同事们的共同努力协作，才使这项工作顺利开展。在此要感谢青岛数码动漫研究院的赵晓春院长，从编写工作的开始阶段，他就给予了亲切的关怀和持久的鼓励，没有他的帮助，这项任务是很难完成的；在编写过程中还得到了同济大学电影研究所杨晓林教授的指点，他在百忙之中为本书作序并提出许多宝贵意见；上海大学数码艺术学院的李敏老师，也为本书提供了很多难得的专业信息资源；东北师范大学外国语学院的王诗戈老师高质量的审校工作，有效保证了本书英语文本的通畅、准确；同时还要感谢本书的责任编辑赵武老师及出版社同仁为本书的编校出版付出的辛勤劳动；最后感谢参与本书编写的东北师范大学美术学院的老师及青岛农业大学艺术与传媒学院的同事们。

作为教学改革的一部分，怎样为艺术类学生开设实用、有效的专业英语课程一直是我们努力探索的课题，这本教材就是我们在教学过程中不断积累的结果。笔者深知书中还存在着许多不完善之处，诚望各界专家学者和朋友们批评指正。

全书具体分工如下：阳泽宇负责编写第 1 章、第 7 章、第 9 章、第 10 章、第 16 章；李艳英负责编写第 4 章；张静负责编写第 2 章、第 3 章、第 5 章、第 6 章；李娟负责编写第 8 章、第 11 章；任庭义负责编写第 12 章；于志恒负责编写第 13 章、第 14 章、第 15 章；王默负责编写第 17 章；苗颖负责编写第 18 章；王诗戈负责各章节的审校；隋华负责课文译稿的校对。

编 者

诚征动画／漫画／游戏设计／数码影像／后期编辑／三维特效／多媒体设计**优秀书稿**

共同打造“中国动漫游戏优秀教材出版工程”

“中国动漫游戏优秀教材出版工程”是国内首家专门定位致力从事动漫游戏教材研发和出版的的机构，由北京电影学院动画学院、中国动画学会及海洋出版社等知名出版机构发起和组建，得到了国家新闻出版总署、中国广播电影电视总局等部门的大力支持。已经推出的“十一五”全国高校动漫游戏专业权威系列教材数十种，全面展示了“最核心的动漫游戏理论”、“最新的数码影像技术”、“最典型的项目应用”，为国内动漫游戏专业提供了一套标准、实用的通用教材，该系列书一经上市，立即受到了业界和广大读者的一致好评，被许多动画专业及相关专业的院校列为指定教材。

中国的动漫游戏教育刚刚起步，动漫游戏等新技术更是日新月异，为了保持我们教材出版的领先性，谨以“开放、诚信、合作、发展”的态度，热诚邀请国内外专家和教师加入到我们的策划和编写队伍中来，我们承诺以“最优秀的编辑出版质量”、“最富创意的营销企划”和“最通畅的发行渠道”对待每一本书稿，保证作者的稿酬收益。另外，依托我们广泛的优势资源和交流网络平台，我们努力促成优秀书稿在海外的出版发行。

投稿热线：(010) 62100088　(010) 62100052　Email：m5_zhaowu@sina.com

教师服务专区

尊敬的各位老师：

真诚感谢您对“中国动漫游戏优秀教材出版工程”的支持，填妥下表，我们将及时为您寄送最新书目和相关资料。

姓名：＿＿＿＿＿＿　性别：＿＿＿＿＿＿　年龄：＿＿＿＿＿＿

联系电话：＿＿＿＿＿＿　Email：＿＿＿＿＿＿

通信地址：＿＿＿＿＿＿　邮编：＿＿＿＿＿＿

学校名称：＿＿＿＿＿＿

教授课程：＿＿＿＿＿＿　班级名称：＿＿＿＿＿＿　学生人数：＿＿＿＿＿＿

教授课程：＿＿＿＿＿＿　班级名称：＿＿＿＿＿＿　学生人数：＿＿＿＿＿＿

教授课程：＿＿＿＿＿＿　班级名称：＿＿＿＿＿＿　学生人数：＿＿＿＿＿＿

教授课程：＿＿＿＿＿＿　班级名称：＿＿＿＿＿＿　学生人数：＿＿＿＿＿＿

您的近期写作计划及主要内容：

社址：北京市海淀区大慧寺路 8 号　网址：http://www.oceanpress.com.cn

技术支持：010-62100052　编辑热线：010-62100088　010-62100023　传真：010-62132549

通信地址：北京市海淀区大慧寺路 8 号海洋出版社教材出版中心　邮编：100081